Resistance and Transformation
On Fairy Tales

Conversation Pieces

A Small Paperback Series from Aqueduct Press
Subscriptions available: www.aqueductpress.com

About the Aqueduct Press
Conversation Pieces Series

The feminist engaged with sf is passionately interested in challenging the way things are, passionately determined to understand how everything works. It is my constant sense of our feminist-sf present as a grand conversation that enables me to trace its existence into the past and from there see its trajectory extending into our future. A genealogy for feminist sf would not constitute a chart depicting direct lineages but would offer us an ever-shifting, fluid mosaic, the individual tiles of which we will probably only ever partially access. What could be more in the spirit of feminist sf than to conceptualize a genealogy that explicitly manifests our own communities across not only space but also time?

Aqueduct's small paperback series, Conversation Pieces, aims to both document and facilitate the "grand conversation." The Conversation Pieces series presents a wide variety of texts, including short fiction (which may not always be sf and may not necessarily even be feminist), essays, speeches, manifestoes, poetry, interviews, correspondence, and group discussions. Many of the texts are reprinted material, but some are new. The grand conversation reaches at least as far back as Mary Shelley and extends, in our speculations and visions, into the continually created future. In Jonathan Goldberg's words, "To look forward to the history that will be, one must look at and retell the history that has been told." And that is what Conversation Pieces is all about.

L. Timmel Duchamp

Jonathan Goldberg, "The History That Will Be" in Louise Fradenburg and Carla Freccero, eds., *Premodern Sexualities* (New York and London: Routledge, 1996)

Conversation Pieces
Volume 78

Resistance and Transformation

On Fairy Tales

by Mari Ness

Published by Aqueduct Press
PO Box 95787
Seattle, WA 98145-2787
www.aqueductpress.com

ISBN: 978-1-61976-195-7

Cover illustration: © Can Stock Photo / stekloduv

Original Block Print of Mary Shelley by Justin Kempton: www.writersmugs.com

Printed in the USA by Applied Digital Imaging

Acknowledgements

"A Pair of Magical Shoes: Variations on Cinderella." First published in Tor.com, May 28, 2015

"Cannibalism and Other Nightmarish Things: Sleeping Beauty." First published in Tor.com, July 2, 2015

"Forbidden Desire and Locked Doors: 'Rapunzel.'" First published in Tor.com, June 9, 2016

"A Fairy Tale Warning: Little Red Riding Hood." First published in Tor.com, February 6, 2017

"Trickery, Social Climbing, and Possibly Fish: Puss in Boots." First published in Tor.com, April 20, 2017

"Enchantment and Distrust: Marie-Jeanne L'Heritier's The Discreet Princess." First published in Tor.com, June 22, 2017

"Two Visions of Transformation: Riquet with the Tuft." First published in Tor.com, July 20, 2017

"Imprisonment and the Fairy Tales of Henriette Julie de Murat." First published in Tor.com, February 15, 2018

"I've Fallen for *Who* Now? The French fairy tale of 'Bearskin.'" First published in Tor.com, Feb 22, 2018

"The Dangers of Propaganda, Flattery, and Violence Toward Cats: 'Prince Desir and Princess Mignone.'" First published in Tor.com, May 31, 2018

"Fairy Tales in Conversation: 'Princess Minute and King Floridor' by the Comte de Caylus." First published in Tor.com, June 14, 2018.

"Unnatural Love and Healing: Charles Perrault's 'Donkey-Skin' and Other Fairy Tales." First published in Tor.com, September 12, 2018.

"A Transformed Woman: Madame d'Aulnoy's 'The White Cat.'" First published in Tor.com, February 14, 2019.

Contents

Introduction

The court of Versailles under Louis XIV could have served as a setting for a fairy tale: dripping with opulence and fulfilled desires; bursting with princesses and princes both wealthy and poor, jealous and generous; and overflowing with nobles who had watched their fortunes rise and fall at the whims of the powerful. (In a very real way: court-iers complained that even the vastness of Versailles did not contain enough rooms to host the number of nobles who wanted or were required to be there.) Masked balls, disguises, and costumes were commonplace; the king's own brother was whispered to play with gender roles and temporarily transform himself. The king himself con-ducted a secret marriage to someone not of his rank.

Naturally, fairy tales sprang up along its edges.

By "edges," I mean the salons—that is, social gather-ings in the homes of the aristocrats and very wealthy, which, during the reign of Louis XIV, slowly turned into centers of education and careful resistance—primar-ily if not exclusively for women, who frequently found themselves excluded from other educational opportuni-ties, including universities and academic societies. The salons allowed these women to pursue their intellectual interests.

Among these interests: fairy tales. Not, I should note, in recording and preserving France's rich oral tradition of folk and fairy tales, or studying the meaning and symbolism behind said tales. That would be for later French scholars. No, the salon fairy tale writers were interested in something else: using the fairy tale to express subversive, revolutionary ideas that could not be expressed openly in the repressive, absolutist court of Louis XIV. And, on a secondary note, using the fairy tale to extend the definition of "literature."

This interest was sparked in part by the works of Italian writers, notably Giovanni Francesco Straparola (1485/1486?–1556/1558?), who published two volumes of fairy tales and fables, *Le Piacevoli Notti,* in 1551 and 1553, and Giambattista Basile (1566–1632), whose *Il Pentamerone,* or *Lo cunto de il cunti overo lo trattenemiento de peccerile*, appeared in 1634 and 1636. Both authors acknowledged that fairy tales were, even then, frequently thought of as children's tales. But Straparola still felt that these tales—which he freely admitted to stealing from other authors—deserved to be written down and preserved. Basile cheerfully included copious amounts of sex, extreme violence, bestiality, cannibalism, and profanity in his versions, in the process making his collection somewhat less than child-friendly.

But both had larger goals than simply preserving or creating fairy tales. They wanted to help establish their "vulgar" languages—Italian and Neapolitan, respectively—as full *literary* languages, equal to Latin and Greek, cultures which had left written collections of myth and what might now be classified as fairy tales. That had already been done to an extent in Italian, but less so in Neapolitan. Basile also took the opportunity to express—under the guise that he was, after all, only writing *fiction*—certain less than friendly and supportive statements about Italian aristocrats, and especially Italian aristocrats and other Italians not fortunate enough to come from Naples.

This proved particularly attractive to many of the attendees of the French salons, many of whom had found themselves in trouble with Louis XIV and his regime for one reason or another, or who came from financially insecure or comparatively marginalized backgrounds—like the talented Catherine Bernard, born to a Huguenot family and therefore never *quite* part of the Catholic establishment, even after her conversion. Others, like the fabulous Henriette Julie de Murat, seemed to positively *revel* in scandal. Not *every* writer of French salon fairy tales was mired in scandal—indeed, the most famous of them, Charles Perrault, lived a nearly irreproachable life from the standpoint of Louis XIV's regime. But many were, and those scandals crept into their remarkable, subversive fairy tales.

The essays in this collection explore some of these remarkable stories, their writers, and the occasional parallel tale from other European cultures. Most originally appeared as part of the *Disney Read-Watch*, which ran on Tor.com between 2015–2017 (with one additional essay appearing in 2018), and *On Fairy Tales*, which ran on Tor.com between 2017–2019. They have been lightly edited to remove repetition and typos in the original versions. I hope you enjoy reading them as much as I enjoyed reading and researching these tales and their writers.

Charles Perrault

A Pair of Magical Shoes:
Variations on *Cinderella*

What do you do when you find yourself downtrodden, turned into a servant by trusted family members, dressed in mud and rags, without, apparently, a friend in the world?

Get some magical footwear—and go dancing.

It's the sort of tale that could easily seize a world. And for the most part, has.

Versions of the Cinderella story date back to ancient times and can be found in nearly every culture. Details vary—sometimes Cinderella is helped by birds, sometimes by magical trees, sometimes by ghosts—as does the footwear. The glass slippers are a comparatively recent—that is, within the last few centuries—addition. Sometimes her family isn't even all that awful. In one of my favorite versions from Italy, the stepsisters, unaware that Cenerentola has a magical bird, are actually friendly to her, offering to bring her to the balls, and upset when she refuses. That tends not to be a particularly popular version, admittedly. Italian composer Gioachino Rossini, for one, found the idea of friendly stepsisters boring, and reinstated the evil stepsisters (who do exist in other Italian versions) along with concocting an extremely convoluted plot regarding the prince, his valet, and his tutor, with everyone running around in disguise. This 1817 version is still performed today.

Probably better known to English speakers, however, are two English translations that also retained the evil stepsisters: *Cinderella*, or "Aschenputtel" (Ash-Fool) as collected and severely edited by the Brothers Grimm, and *Cinderella, or the Glass Slipper*, as elegantly penned by Charles Perrault.

The Grimm version is, well, *grim* (I'm neither the first nor last to use this pun). It starts off on a sad note ("A rich man's wife became sick,") and before we're even out of the first paragraph, someone's dead. This is followed by weeping and mourning, magical trees, more crying, hunting for lentils in ashes, the destruction of a completely innocent pigeon coop, the killing of a perfectly innocent (non-magical) tree, one girl cutting off her toe, another girl cutting off her heel, drops of blood everywhere, and pigeons flying down to pluck out eyes. Very cheerful.

What's remarkable about this version is Cinderella herself: although often perceived as a passive character, here, she is a magical creature with gifts of her own. Her tears, spilled over a hazel branch, allow that branch to grow into a magical tree. When Cinderella needs something, she heads out to the tree, shakes it, and receives it—no waiting around for a magical fairy godmother to help. When her evil stepmother sets impossible tasks with lentils and peas, Cinderella heads outside and summons birds to help, and they do. This is the sort of heroine who *deserves* a prince. Though, to counter that, this is not a particularly kindly or forgiving Cinderella: the text establishes that Cinderella can control birds, to an extent, but when pigeons swoop down to pluck out her stepsisters' eyes (the text cheerfully says they deserve this), she does nothing. Also remarkable: in this version, Cinderella goes to the ball three times, and her shoe is not fragile glass but firm gold, a shoe provided by her magical tree.

Some of this stemmed from a certain anti-French sentiment on the part of the Grimms, who were, after all, collecting their tales only a decade or so after the Napoleonic Wars and the subsequent social and political upheavals in Germany. This meant, in part, an emphasis on qualities considered particularly German: piety, modesty, and hard work (the Grimm version emphasizes that for all of Cinderella's magical trees and bird summoning abilities, not something exactly associated with Christian tradition, she remains pious and good), as well as a rejection of certain elements considered especially "French," such as fairies.

With Aschenputtel in particular, the Grimms were reacting to the other famous literary version of the tale: *Cinderella, or the Glass Slipper,* by Charles Perrault.

Who in turn was reacting to the fairy-tale traditions of 17th-century French salons—tales written by authors frequently on the margins of high society, who used fairy tales to examine aristocratic French society (they did not have a lot of interest in the peasants), and in particular, the inequities and limitations often faced by aristocratic women. Or, occasionally, to sneak in a few BDSM scenes right past French censors and others with delicate sensibilities.

Exactly what Perrault thought about the kinky stuff is not known, but he had definite ideas about fairy tales.

Unlike many of his fellow French salon fairy-tale writers, his life was virtually sedate. And much unlike most of them, he greatly admired the court of Louis XIV, where he had a distinguished career. From his position within the court, Perrault argued that Louis XIV's enlightened rule had made France the greatest country and civilization of all time. That career was all the more remarkable since Perrault and his direct supervisor, Jean-Baptiste Colbert, unlike most courtiers and high ranking officials, were not born into the French aristocracy, and were recognized for their talents, not their blood.

Perhaps because of that success, Perrault's version of *Cinderella* specifically focuses on a middle-class heroine without, apparently, a touch of aristocratic blood, who rises into the court largely by force of her inner talents—and a touch of magic. The story contains delightful little tidbits of French fashion and hairdressing issues (fortunately, Cinderella's talents include hair styling—and she has excellent taste, something you always want in your soon-to-be-princess). These not only give a very realistic touch to the story, but firmly set the story in a very real Paris, making its focus on a heroine without a title all the more remarkable—especially since Perrault's target audience was the minor nobility as well as the growing upper-middle class.

His version is not precisely free of snobbery and concern for class—Perrault clarifies that the king's son invites only "persons of fashion" (read: people with money, or people with the ability to fake having money) to his ball, not the "all the ladies of the land" that appear in later tellings and reinterpretations. This also holds true for the great glass-slipper tryouts: Perrault specifically states that the slipper is tested, not on everyone, but on princesses, duchesses, and court ladies. Cinderella gets a try only after she asks—and only because the man holding the shoe thinks she's handsome. Sure, you can jump out of your social class—if you have the right social connections, the right clothes, the right looks, and, well, the right shoe.

Perrault's emphasis on fashion brings up another point: Cinderella succeeds in large part because she has the social skills needed by upper-class women: excellent taste in fashion (to the point where her stepsisters beg for her assistance), politeness, and, of course, the ability to dance gracefully. In other words, she succeeds because she is supporting the status quo—and an aristocracy that recognizes her good qualities (once she's properly dressed). This is in stark contrast to other French fairy tales, where fine clothing does not always lead to acceptance, and the protagonists find themselves struggling to prove their worth. But it is also an emphasis on how the structures in place help *reward* women.

But for all its emphasis on approved gender roles, and for all his admiration of the French court, the story still has a touch—just a touch—of subversion in the tale, since Cinderella is not a princess. This may not seem like much, but it's another contrast with the fairy tales he's reacting to, many of which insist on marriage within the same social class. The original version of *Beauty and the Beast,* a long, tedious novella which we'll be discussing later, goes to great lengths to emphasize that a prince can only marry a princess, and vice versa. Perrault, unlike that author, admired social climbers.

And, like other social climbers in the French aristocracy, Cinderella makes sure to reward family members. The stepsisters here don't have their eyes gouged out, or find their feet dripping with blood: after flinging themselves at Cinderella's feet, they are carefully married off to noblemen. This not only emphasizes her goodness, but also ensures that at least two members of her court will have reason to be grateful to her—even if their husbands, perhaps, will not. Though I'm not entirely without hope—the Perrault version is also the start of the tradition that the younger of the two evil stepsisters is just a little less evil. It's another nice humanizing touch, reminding us that not all villains are equally evil, and suggests that just maybe the noble that married her didn't have a terrible time of it after all.

Speaking of evil villains, though, in this version, we never do find out what happened to the stepmother afterwards. Presumably her only problem is trying to find a replacement scullery maid who also knows how to style hair really well. Get ready to pay out some big wages, oh evil stepmother.

But Perrault's version did not become famous because of the stepmother, or the stepsisters, but because of the little magical details thrown into the story: the pumpkin, the transformed mice, and of course, that famous glass slipper leading to a happy ending. It's almost enough to make even the most determined revolutionary raise a glass to the reign of Louis XIV.

Almost.

Cannibalism and Other Nightmarish Things: *Sleeping Beauty*

Stories of enchanted sleepers stretch well back into ancient times. In European mythology, they appear in multiple forms: stories of fabled warriors resting under mountains or on enchanted isles until it is time for them to return to serve their city or country in the time of greatest need—though if England hasn't *actually* faced its greatest need yet, I shudder to think what it would take to bring King Arthur back to its shores. Stories of sleeping saints. Stories of women sleeping in caves, in mountains, and in towers.

Unchanged. Static. Beautiful. Waiting, perhaps, for a kiss from a prince.

The literary version of *Sleeping Beauty* probably originates from Giambattista Basile's "Sun, Moon, and Talia," one of a collection of tales published posthumously in 1634. It's a cheerful little story of a girl who in this version is not *quite* a princess, only the daughter of a lord, who, after pricking her finger on a bit of flax and swooning, is placed on a lovely canopied bed in a nice country mansion. Naturally, a king rides up, as they do (Basile calls this "by chance"), and goes into the mansion without asking, because, well, king. Basile sums up the next bit quite nicely:

> Crying aloud, he beheld her charms and felt his blood course hotly through his veins. He lifted her in his arms, and carried her to a bed, where he gathered the first fruits of love. Leaving her on the bed, he returned to his own kingdom, where, in the pressing business of his realm, he for a time thought no more about this incident.

Notice what little detail is left out of these three sentences? Yeah, that's right: ***the waking up part.***

Talia even brings this up later, pointing out that the king had "taken possession while she was asleep." The romance is giving me chills here. Between this and Snow White, I'm beginning to have some serious doubts about fairy-tale kings and their choice in sexual partners, is all I'm saying.

Though, to be fair, to this king it was the sort of incident that he could easily forget about.

Nah, I don't want to be fair.

After this bit, it will probably not surprise anyone to read that Talia manages to sleep right through her pregnancy, which worries me—I can't help but feel that she did not get proper nutrition during any of this. What does wake her up: her twin babies sucking on her fingers—since one of them sucks out the little piece of flax that put her to sleep. Talia handles the whole waking up to find baby twins crawling all over her very well, I must say; it's an example to us all.

Until, that is, the king remembers that oh, yes, *that* happened, decides to visit his rape victim, and after seeing his kids decides to tell Talia the truth. It goes remarkably well:

> When she heard this, their friendship was knitted with tighter bonds, and he remained with her for a few days.

What friendship? you might be asking, given that this is the first time they've actually, you know, *spoken*, but there's no time to focus on this because the story has a *lot* of cannibalism, betrayal, and infidelity to get to and not all that much time to get to it.

Oh, did I not mention that in this version, Prince Charming isn't just a rapist, he's an *already married rapist*, who has the nerve to complain after cheating on her with Talia that his wife didn't bring him a dowry when he got married? Granted, he says this just as his wife is serving him up what she thinks is a dish that includes the delicate tender flesh of his little twin children—it's that kind of story—so clearly, the dowry issue isn't the only problem here, but this king is a total jerk, is what I'm saying.

Also, Talia/Sleeping Beauty ends up doing a striptease for this wife, partly to make sure that her jewel encrusted dress doesn't get burned up, because that's important. Also the story ends with an implication that Talia, this king, and their kids end up in a rather incestuous foursome, which, *this story.*

Additional detail that you probably don't want to know: this version strongly implies that Talia aka Sleeping Beauty has no nipples. You're welcome.

Also two fairies are flitting around the story, but I must say, they don't help much.

Astonishingly enough, when Perrault came across this story about sixty years later, his first thought was apparently not "So, this is mildly appalling," or even "Why is this guy so hung up about this dowry thing when he might be *actually eating his own kids,*" but rather, "Wow, this is *exactly* the sort of story I want to tell the French court *and* my kids!"

Which he did.

But not without making some changes. Perrault believed strongly in the French aristocracy, and whatever else can be said about the Talia story, it is not a particularly pro-aristocratic tale. The most sympathetic and heroic figure in it is the cook, who, as a bonus, is also the one character—apart from the fairies—who also manages to keep all of his clothes on and not participate in adultery, cannibalism, burning people alive, or incest, like, you go, cook, you go! Perrault liked tales featuring upper-middle-class characters and social climbers, and stories that emphasized the benefits of an aristocratic system, but was less fond of stories where the main hero turns out to be the happily married cook. He was also, apparently, not fond of stripteases in his fairy tales.

So Perrault tweaked the story. The fairies were inserted much earlier on, adding a touch of magic and fate. To eliminate the adultery, the king's wife was changed into the king's mother, and to more or less justify all of the cannibalism, she was further transformed into an ogress. This change doesn't entirely work, given that it brings up all *kinds* of questions, like why, exactly, did the previous king marry an ogre in the first place? Presumably for political reasons, but what sort of alliance was anyone hoping to get from this? Was this meant as a reference to one of the many political alliances Perrault had witnessed in his years at Louis XIV's court? If so, which one? Enquiring minds want to know. And, well, this makes the prince half ogre, right? How is *that* working, and did Sleeping Beauty ever notice this? And did the prince ever warn Sleeping Beauty before finally bringing her to his castle that, hey, my mother is a bit of an ogre? And did Sleeping Beauty—who, in this version, is just a teenager—realize that in this case, the prince was serious, and not just speaking in metaphors?

And speaking of oddities, in this version, after the fairy puts all of the servants and nobles at the court to sleep so that Sleeping Beauty won't feel alone when she wakes up, the king and queen just…ride off. Was this an actual enchantment, or a method for getting rid of some troublesome court attendants and a few unskilled cooks for a hundred years or so without killing them? Especially since the fairy knew full well that a handsome prince—well, ok, a half ogre prince, if we're quibbling—would be right there at Sleeping Beauty's side when she awoke? You decide.

In more positive changes, the prince in this version doesn't even kiss Sleeping Beauty to wake her up: he just kneels in front of her. This is apparently enough to make her fall in love with him the second she wakes up, like, ***see how much not raping women can help you out romantically, guys,*** although Perrault kinda softens this by pointing out that the fairy had probably given Sleeping Beauty some delightful dreams of the prince while she was sleeping, so she's pretty prepared for the whole marriage thing.

One interesting detail in Perrault's version: the court failed to invite the old fairy who curses Sleeping Beauty to the christening not because the fairy was evil—but because the court believed that the fairy was trapped in a tower, much like Rapunzel, or Sleeping Beauty later. A reflection, perhaps, of Perrault's observations of Louis XIV's court, where princesses and grand duchesses could disappear for years, mostly forgotten, before making rather less than triumphant returns?

The second half of the story—the bit with the ogre—certainly does seem to reflect a bit of court society, first when the prince, later king, attempts to hide his marriage from his mother the ogre queen, a nod, perhaps, to the many secret court marriages that Perrault had witnessed, and later when the rival queens—Sleeping Beauty and her ogre mother-in-law—play games of murder and deception against each other in the king's absence. It's also an example—unintended, perhaps—of just what can go wrong when the king leaves his court for a foreign war, and an illustration—intended, almost certainly—of the king as the source of order and safety.

Not that the story is all about the aristocracy. Perrault also added an adorable puppy. We don't really get to hear much about the puppy, but I like the thought that Sleeping Beauty has a dog beside her for the entire century. It's sweet.

This still wasn't sweet enough for the Grimm Brothers, who, in a departure from their usual acceptance of blood and gore, decided to axe the second part of the story the bit with the ogre and the eating of small children, typically a Grimm staple—though they did leave in the idea of dead princes hanging from the briar roses outside the castle, as a warning, perhaps, to those who might want to cross boundaries. In an unusual twist, they added more fairies—typically, the Grimms liked to remove French fairies from every tale they could, but in this case they had thirteen fairies to Perrault's eight—twelve or seven good fairies to a single bad one. They also made their Briar-Rose just a touch younger—fifteen, to Perrault's sixteen.

And as a final touch, they added a kiss to wake the sleeping princess.

Andrew Lang preferred the longer, richer Perrault version, including that tale in *The Blue Fairy Book*. But despite this, the Grimm version was the one to persist and the version Disney chose to work with. Perhaps because it suggested that everything really could change with a kiss.

Gabrielle-Suzanne Barbot de Villeneuve

Marriage Can Be Monstrous, or Wondrous: The Origins of *Beauty and the Beast*

Technically speaking, *Beauty and the Beast* is not *quite* a tale as old as time—time, after all, more or less got going right after the Big Bang, well before anyone was telling any fairy tales at all. But in human terms, the story of *Beauty and the Beast* is very old indeed, with literary roots stretching well back into antiquity, making this arguably the second oldest story in this essay series, after the stories of Hercules.

Which makes it all the more remarkable that in the original literary version, the Beast isn't a Beast at all, although some people *think* he is.

That version was first written down by second century author Apuleius (sometimes referred to as Lucius Apuleius Madaurensis) in a book called *Metamorphoses*, better known today as *The Golden Ass*. It's the one novel that has survived from the Roman period, thus garnering significant attention, both for the overall novel, and for the story told in its center, that of *Cupid and Psyche*.

Images of Cupid—or Eros in Greek—and Psyche predate the novel, suggesting that Apuleius may not have invented the original story. Since we have no other written sources, however, it's possible that he did create a new story, inspired by the images he saw on vases and paintings. Certainly the Cupid of the story is not quite like the Cupid or Eros that appears in other tales—even if Apuleius' Cupid soon became a major subject of later artworks.

Regardless, the final result is almost pure fairy tale—though the fairies in this tale are Roman deities, and the enchanted realms visited by Psyche are inhabited not by fairies, but by the dead. Otherwise, the elements here are all staples of the later European fairy tales. Psyche is the youngest and the most beautiful of three sisters; she gains the enmity of a supernatural mother-in-law; and to win her husband, she must complete a series of impossible tasks: separating out a huge mound of grains and beans (as later seen in some versions of *Cinderella* and various tales featuring grateful animals); gathering golden wool from killer sheep; gathering water from the river Styx; and visiting the underworld to gather a beauty remedy from Proserpina, queen of the dead, something that—thanks to Psyche's curiosity and her own desire to be beautiful—almost kills her by sending her into a torpor.

(Incidentally, Apuleius, I don't mean to overreact here, but are you actually trying to suggest that the best way for women to become or regain their beauty is for them to spend some time in a coma? Great.)

As the tale begins, Psyche, despite her beauty—so extraordinary that people are worshiping her instead of Venus, goddess of love and beauty—cannot find a husband. Distressed, her father consults the oracle of Delphi, despite the oracle's historical predilection for saying incredibly depressing things. Living right down to its reputation, the oracle announces that Psyche is destined to marry a monster that neither gods nor humans can resist. From this and other ancient tales, I have no idea why people didn't just burn the oracle of Delphi down to the ground, but I digress. Anyway, everyone responds to this cheery announcement by leaving her on the top of a mountain, dressed in funeral clothes. Very supportive, everyone. Very supportive.

Fortunately for Psyche, she is whisked away by the nice gentle West Wind to a magical palace of gold filled with invisible servants ready to fulfill her every command. The otherwise lovely 1855 translation by Thomas Bulfinch glosses over the next part, where Psyche, worried about her virginity, finds her marriage thoroughly consummated in the darkness. She spends the next few days crying, as do her sisters; finally, her mysterious husband agrees that her sisters can visit. Psyche, like her later Victorian translators, initially decides to gloss over the situation, but in a later visit, tells her sisters the truth: she has never seen her husband. They freak out.

The original Latin has a side note here, left out of some translations, where the sisters complain that their own husbands don't respect them and then detail just why, recounting a horror show of marital captivity, refusal to pay bills, forced labor, and sexual dissatisfaction. For all that this is in the end a story arguing for love, and arguing that spouses can fall in love with each other after marriage, it's also a story well aware that many marriages in the Roman Empire went badly for women.

Anyway, sidenote over, the sisters persuade Psyche that she must—she *must*—see her husband's face, and although by this point, she is in love with him, she tries—and in trying, loses him, at least until she can complete those impossible tasks and earn his love. Naturally, he blames her, and she is cast out into the world to wander looking for him.

She's pregnant.

Love—that is, Cupid in this story—not always the nicest guy. Sure, he claims he doesn't have a choice here, but do we believe him?

Making matters just a touch worse, the entire *narrative* point of including this story in *The Golden Ass* is to convince a young girl that really, getting raped by pirates is just fine and will work out great for her.

This part of the novel ended up passing through multiple oral and literary traditions. It eventually appeared in several languages in different forms, most notably in *East of the Sun, West of the Moon* and *The Dark King. East of the Sun, West of the Moon* kept most of the elements of the original tale, just changing the unknown monster into a white bear, and changing the tasks—and who has to complete said tasks. *The Dark King,* a Sicilian version, changed Psyche into one of the poorest peasants in Sicily, if still beautiful, placed the enchanted palace well underground, and primly did not marry the girl and her invisible, enchanted husband off until the very end of the tale—after he'd tossed her out to wander Sicily in rags. Indeed, in these stories, generally the most decent of the husbands turn out to be the ones enchanted into the shapes of beasts, the men that have to be rescued by love. It was perhaps these examples that caught the attention of Gabrielle-Suzanne Barbot de Villeneuve (1695–1755), the first to write the story of *Beauty and the Beast* as we know it today in literary form, as a long, tedious novella (very long, do not read) contained in her even longer, even more tedious work, *Les Contes marins ou la jeune Americaine* (1740) (again, very long, don't read).

De Villeneuve came from the minor nobility and led an unconventional life. She married a lieutenant colonel who also came from the minor nobility. After his death, she moved to Paris and, eventually, into the house of Prosper Jolyot de Crébillon, a poet left bitter after years at the court of Versailles They did not marry. Instead, following the advice of his son, the novelist Claude Prosper Jolyot de Crébillon, de Villenueve turned to writing to supplement what was apparently a small or nearly non-existent income. A few years after the younger de Crébillon gave her this advice, he ended up in a French jail for writing a novel believed to contain attacks on certain high ranking French officials; he was later exiled from Paris for writing an erotic political novel. Undaunted, de Villeneuve kept writing.

Her experiences, and quite possibly those of the de Crébillons, left her with both a certain cynicism and an awareness of the issues faced by aristocratic women of the upper and lower nobility. Both of these appear in the very first pages of her novella, which note the vicissitudes of fortune. When Beauty's supposed father loses his fortune, the hoped-for marriages of his six daughters all completely collapse. They may be beautiful and charming, but without money, that is not enough. De Villeneuve had seen enough of life to be aware of how many people respond to misfortune. Not well, even if, as in this case, the misfortune involves downgrading to a "country" life, which means—gasp—woolen gowns and the sons having to do—more gasps—*physical labor* (not detailed)—all while keeping a harpsichord and various fine instruments.

The fine instruments, by the way, baffle me. De Villeneuve tells us that the family's mansion burns down and they lose everything and have to move to, and I quote, "the saddest abode in the world," and almost everybody has to work as a servant (the older sisters just cry) and yet, a few paragraphs later, Beauty is happily playing away on various fine and, yes, even for that era, very expensive instruments. You'd think that since they saved the harpsichord, they also could have managed to bring along a servant, but apparently not. Moving along.

From here, the familiar elements enter the story: the rose, the enchanted castle, the infuriated beast, and Beauty traveling to the castle to save her supposed father, with one unexpected twist: in this version, the story does not end when Beauty kisses the Beast and restores him to his rightful place, but goes on. And on. And on. And then, on. And then, just when you think it can't possibly continue for any longer, it goes on.

And on.

It's long, is what I'm saying, even if it's filled with fascinating little details. I thoroughly approve of the way everyone sips chocolate instead of coffee or tea, for instance, in the morning, and sometimes in the evening. I also love the way Beauty, in the midst of her own issues, stops everything to watch palace revolutions in Istanbul through a magical window. And as tedious as her story is, I love the portrait of the warrior queen, who appears in the second, much longer part of the story, caught between concern for her son and the job she must do of saving the kingdom. It's a fascinating tale, especially since she's not just a warrior queen, but also a major snob, convinced that Beauty doesn't deserve to marry her son, since Beauty is (supposedly) the daughter of a merchant. Oh, the queen is certainly *grateful,* and she'll happily toss Beauty off to some noble or other, you understand, but not *that* grateful.

But this isn't just a tale of snobbery, chocolate, transformation, and revolutions in Istanbul: *Beauty and the Beast* is, above all, the story of *working women* and the choices they must make. Nearly every woman in this story, including the aristocrats, has a job, and every woman struggles, not always successfully, with balancing work, life, marriage, and children. The failures, when they happen, are disastrous for themselves and their children alike. (And also for the poor countries overrun by wars in the middle of all this.)

The human warrior queen chooses her job—and is forced to watch her beloved son be transformed into a beast (and, in an even more dreadful moment, *come close to marrying a merchant's daughter;* I hope you all appreciate how awful she thinks she is, although to its credit, the text disagrees). The fairy queen chooses her family—and finds herself imprisoned, forced to change back and forth into a serpent, and separated from her daughter, who ends up with the merchant. It is brutal, and compassionate, a tale of the difficult choices faced by women and the restrictions and rules placed upon them that forces them to make these choices in the first place. It helps, too, that both women are deeply flawed characters who make mistakes—but who then do everything in their limited power to correct them. Perhaps not surprisingly, the least tolerable character in the story is not the main villain (another woman) but the one older woman, a fairy, who does not have children, and who does not face quite the same heartbreaking choices, even as she runs around trying to fix matters.

Also, in the story: a *lot* of caressing, which at one point almost seems to be heading right into a major incestuous orgy (it doesn't) and eventually led me to start shouting STOP CARESSING EACH OTHER AND JUST GET ON WITH IT at the book.

Almost inevitably, whenever I bring any of this up, especially the warrior queen, the chocolate, and the caressing, people want to read the story. And I can only respond with, *don't*. It's tedious. Very, very, tedious. It was left to another French writer, Jeanne-Marie Leprince de Beaumont, to salvage the story and turn it—almost—into the version we know today in English. I say almost, because although several English collections use straightforward translations of de Beaumont's version, others use Andrew Lang's version, a mix of both de Beaumont and de Villeneuve, which first appeared in *The Blue Fairy Book* in 1889.

De Beaumont, unlike de Villeneuve, was born into straitened circumstances and began working as a teacher at a young age to support herself. She managed to obtain a job as a singing teacher in a ducal household, where she married a Monsieur de Beaumont. The marriage was a disaster—de Beaumont allegedly picked up a venereal disease and liked orgies, which shocked his less allegedly prim and proper wife—and the marriage was annulled after only two years, something highly unusual for the period. The following year de Beaumont fled to England, seeking employment as a governess. The position paid poorly, and she began to write, a career she continued even after a second, more successful marriage.

Her version of *Beauty and the Beast* was a moralistic one written for children, originally published in 1756 in *Le Magasin des Enfants,* which published several of her tales. De Beaumont ruthlessly excised all of the post-kiss parts of de Villeneuve's tale, and ruthlessly trimmed quite a lot of the pre-kiss parts of de Villeneuve's tale as well—no one in her story has time to sip chocolate or watch palace revolutions. De Beaumont also removed several of Beauty's supposed brothers and sisters, creating a more manageable family of three sons and three daughters, and focused her story not on the issues facing women, but on the importance of judging by reality, not appearances, a lesson she herself had apparently learned the hard way. Her story urges girls to value virtue over beauty and wit, another lesson she herself had apparently learned the hard way. She also turned Beauty's envious sisters into stone statues, in an echo of the fate of the sisters in *The Golden Ass*—while reassuring children that yes, the sisters *could* become human again, if they learned to recognize their faults.

She made one other significant change: in her version, Beauty remains the daughter of a merchant. (In the de Villeneuve version, Beauty is raised by a merchant family, but turns out to be the daughter of a fairy and a king, fortunately enough because did I mention the snobbery? Oh, yes, the snobbery.) De Beaumont was well aware that young middle-class girls of her time, like aristocratic ones, could also be married off to men they barely knew. Her tale speaks to those fears, assuring them that—if they were virtuous and obedient, they could find happiness in marriage.

I bring all this up because, for valid reasons, *Beauty and the Beast* has often been read as a tale urging women to look, not just beyond ugly appearances, but ugly behavior (in both versions, after all, the Beast imprisons Beauty), a tale that assures women that they have the power to transform beasts into men, a tale often contrasted with *Bluebeard*, which clearly states that yes, if a man has had several wives *and* has a weird look *and* gives you strange instructions about keys and doors, running away is, hands-down, your best option, whatever you may think about the bonds of marriage, especially if you do not have brothers who can rescue you in time.

Whoops, I went off track there. As said, this reading has a certain validity, especially since the Beasts in both versions of this tale are, well, *Beasts*—terrifying not just Beauty, but her father. Her sisters, however wrong their motives, are not entirely wrong when they ask Beauty not to return to him. And yes, Beauty's kiss does transform the Beast.

But I would argue that the tales themselves are more complicated than that. That these are tales written by women who knew the dangers of abusive men and understood that their world did not always offer easy choices or simple answers. That in de Villeneuve's tale, abusers appear everywhere, sometimes in disguise, sometimes not; that law and duty, and honor and virtue can often be difficult. That in de Villeneuve's tales, the choices faced by women—including Beauty—are not so simple. And that de Beaumont, who insisted so strongly on virtue over appearance had been married to a man she considered a monster and she had survived. She wanted her readers to know that they could survive as well, and that may be the greatest message that shines through both tales.

Charlotte-Rose de Caumont de La Force

Forbidden Desire and Locked Doors:
Rapunzel

Stories of maidens locked into towers or behind walls litter European folklore, appearing in fairy tales, saints' lives, and dubious histories and chronicles. In part, these tales echoed the real life experiences of women locked behind walls for one reason or another. Some women went willingly. Convent life, for instance, could offer not just a religious experience and spiritual comfort, but also educational and artistic opportunities for many women. Other women did not.

But even the strictest convents and prisons did not completely remove these women from the world of men. Not even in the case of arguably the most famous fictional woman to be trapped in a tower, Rapunzel.

Rapunzel was collected by the Grimms for their first edition of *Children and Household Tales*, initially published in 1812. Like "Little Briar Rose," it is a tale that came to the Grimms through the French aristocracy, in this case through the story "Parslinette," published by Charlotte-Rose de Caumont de La Force in 1697. The daughter of a marquis, she was the protégé of one of Louis XIV's mistresses, Madame de Maintenon, who would later, very secretly, marry Louis XIV. De La Force used this relationship to become a maid of honor first to the queen and later to the dauphine of France. As a maid of honor, she proceeded to have multiple love affairs and a marriage with a very much younger man that his shocked family managed to have annulled—even though the marriage had been approved by the king himself.

In between the multiple love affairs, she wrote violent and sexy historical romances published to great acclaim, fairy tales, and poems primly described as "impious." The poems were too impious for Louis XIV, who ignored de La Force's relationship with his mistress and sent the author to a convent. Trapped behind walls, she continued to write. "Parslinette" was one of the first stories she penned behind convent walls.

"Parslinette" is a story of forbidden desire. It starts with the story of a woman craving the parsley that grows in a fairy's garden and can be found nowhere else—de la Force assures us that the parsley in question is extremely delectable. Her husband sneaks into the garden through a door that just happens to be open for a moment. When he is—inevitably—discovered, the only thing that the fairy will accept in payment for the stolen parsley is his child. It's both a familiar folktale motif, from a tale that de La Force almost certainly heard as a child, and a reflection of the reality de la Force knew all too well: walled off gardens, foods restricted to the powerful who lived behind those walls, and punishments far outweighing the original offense.

The fairy takes the child and walls her away in a tower another reflection of a historical reality de la Force, who had watched children, legitimate and illegitimate, taken from mothers and hidden away in convents or in secret homes, knew all too well. It was exactly how her own mentor, Madame de Maintenon, had come to the attention of Louis XIV—as one of the discreet governesses of his illegitimate children. It's a delightful life, filled with luxuries, and Parslinette is never bored or lonely, but happy. That is, until a prince overhears her singing voice, and comes to the tower.

She's terrified. To quote from Jack Zipes' translation:

> …for she remembered that she had heard
> there were men who could kill with their eyes,
> and this man's looks were very dangerous.

She does not let him in. It's important, I think, to note at this point that although Parslinette has spent her life locked away in a tower, she's not completely naïve or uneducated: the text makes a point of telling us that she reads, a lot. It's possible that she heard about the men who could kill with their eyes from the fairy, but the fairy has mostly left her alone in the tower. It's equally possible that she learned this in a book.

It gets a bit worse. The prince tricks his way up into the tower:

> Then he bowed down before Parslinette and
> embraced her knees with ardor, to persuade
> her of his love. But she was afraid.

Well, maybe if you hadn't gone directly for her legs, dude. Or said "Bonjour!" first. Either way.

In any case, they are married—well, sorta—in the next few sentences. I say sorta because the only two people present for this "wedding" are the prince and Parslinette, which leads me to the suspicion that just possibly this ceremony was not all that legal. Or religious. She quickly becomes pregnant:

Since she had no idea what her condition signified, she was upset. Although the prince knew, he did not want to explain it to her for fear of frightening her.

Ok, so maybe she didn't learn all that much from books.

Also, dude! What's better, scaring her a bit now, or, you know, LETTING HER KNOW THAT A SMALL HUNGRY CHILD WILL BE PART OF HER LIFE IN A FEW MONTHS?

Anyway. Her pregnancy gets Parslinette kicked out of the tower in yet another echo of real life experiences that de La Force had personally witnessed: women driven from luxurious homes after becoming pregnant illicitly, giving birth behind convent walls, in secret homes, in distant towns, or even in the streets.

The fairy also makes the prince throw himself off the top of the tower (yay!) which makes him go blind (hmm). This doesn't do quite as much to keep him from Parslinette as I was kinda hoping; after various adventures that at least do include turning him into stone (and then, alas, turning him back into a human), he, Parslinette, and their twin kids end up back in his father's palace and live happily ever after—this, despite the fact that Parslinette is not a princess, or even, apparently, of noble birth.

That, too, was something de La Force had personally witnessed—a secret wedding between a king and a woman of non-royal birth. Which is to say, for a so-called fairy tale, "Parslinette" is oddly grounded in reality—even if one of its major characters is a fairy.

That very reality was to give the Grimms a bit of trouble when they collected the tale a little over one hundred years later, apparently unaware that their *Rapunzel* was nothing more than an abridged version of de La Force's stylish literary tale. It's impossible to know for sure, but given that the Grimms were primarily interested in preserving German culture, it seems unlikely that they would have bothered to preserve—and later clean up—a story from France. And yet, that's basically what the version of *Rapunzel* in the first edition of Grimms' *Household Tales* is. A few elements have been changed—the mother now wants rapunzel, instead of parsley, giving the protagonist a different name, and the list of luxuries that Parslinette enjoys in her tower, as well as that important note about her education, is gone. As is the bit where the prince briefly turns into stone, sigh. But otherwise, everything is the same: the mother longing for a green plant from a fairy garden; her husband getting that plant; the girl locked in the tower and letting down her hair to let the prince up; the angry fairy tossing him from the tower, causing him to lose his eyesight; the twins, the happy ending.

And oh, yes, that pregnancy.

The Grimm brothers kept the pregnancy, and Rapunzel's confusion about it, in that first edition of *Household Tales*—an edition *not* meant for children. Children apparently read it anyway (go, kids, go!) and subsequent editions took out many of the elements deemed objectionable.

Including illicit pregnancies.

In later editions, the Grimms did take the opportunity to add one bit of explanatory detail: in their retelling, the prince loses his eyesight because he just happened to fall on some thorns. Their other changes, however, focused on making the story more "suitable" for children and also more "German." As a result, by the seventh edition (1857), their version could be kindly called "confused." For instance, the text alternatively describes the antagonist as both a "fairy" (a creature from French folklore, not the German folklore the Grimms wanted to emphasize), and a "sorceress" (considerably scarier, and also, not a French fairy). The terms aren't *too* far off, but where the original French story focused on the enchantments and luxuries available to the enclosed Parslinette, the Grimm version focuses on the entrapment and isolation, transforming the somewhat more ambiguous figure of the French tale into a figure of evil.

Rapunzel no longer asks the fairy, or the witch, why her clothes are suddenly tight; she instead asks the witch why she is so much harder to pull up than the prince. In the first version, of course, no one has bothered to tell her anything about pregnancy. In the second version, Rapunzel looks at best careless and at worst lacking all common sense. If she'd been established as someone who speaks without thinking, it might have worked. But the story gives no indication of that: we're instead left to assume that Rapunzel is a bit of an airhead. Or that her hair has just dragged all common sense out of her. Whichever. Her twins appear literally out of nowhere in the final two sentences of the story.

This was the version Andrew Lang turned to as he began collecting the stories for *The Red Fairy Book* (1890). His version removed the twins entirely and cleared up the confusing references to fairy and sorceress, instead using "witch." This became the most familiar version to English readers, although readers can also find translations of both the French version and various Grimm versions.

But the power of the tale, I think, in whatever version, comes not from the name of the protagonist, or Rapunzel's pregnancy, or even the image of Rapunzel letting her golden hair drape down from a tiny window in her tower. Rather, it's the way that all versions, from French to English, reflect a very real historical circumstance: women who, for one reason or another, retreated behind stone walls and into towers, voluntarily and involuntarily. That Parslinette/Rapunzel just happens to retreat into a tower (often used as a phallic symbol) guarded by a woman only adds to this power.

A Fairy Tale Warning:
Little Red Riding Hood

In most of the pictures, she looks so innocent. So young. So *adorable,* with her little red hood and basket. (Though in some adult costuming contexts, she looks more than ready to party.) In some illustrations she's six, at most, in others, ten—old enough to be sent on errands through the forest, especially errands of mercy to a beloved grandmother.

In the original tale, she dies.

That first literary version of *Little Red Riding Hood* was penned by Perrault, who included it with ten other stories in his *Histoires ou Contes du Temps passé*, or *Les Contes de ma Mère l'Oye* (Mother Goose stories), originally published in 1697. Perrault stood out from his fellow salon fairy-tale writers in several important respects. Unlike nearly all of them, his life was mostly scandal free. He did marry a much younger woman later in life, but that was hardly unheard of for the period, and nothing compared to his fellow fairy-tale writers, who were frequently involved in court intrigues, adultery, and (alleged) treason. And unlike nearly all of them, he enjoyed a highly successful career at Versailles, a position that enabled him to establish and patronize academies dedicated to the arts—perhaps at least partly thanks to his ability to avoid scandal.

Presumably because of this highly successful career, he was one of the very few French salon fairy-tale writers who thoroughly approved of Louis XIV and had no interest in critiquing royal absolutism. With the sole exception of the king in *Donkey-Skin*, his kings are not evil. Helpless against the powers of evil fairies and the hunger of ogres, perhaps—as in *Sleeping Beauty*—but not evil, or overthrown, or manipulated, or deceived. For Perrault, kings and aristocrats are not threats who need to be removed, or obstacles to happiness, but figures his characters aspire to become.

Above all, Perrault differed from most of his fellow fairy-tale writers, with the exception of his niece, Marie-Jeanne L'Heritier, in that he was not born into the aristocracy. Granted, he was hardly a peasant. His family was wealthy enough to afford excellent educations for their sons and purchase government positions for them. Perrault was skilled and talented enough to attract the attention and patronage of the Minister of Finances, Jean-Baptiste Colbert. Like Perrault, Colbert had not been born an aristocrat, but he eventually purchased a baronetcy and became one. Perhaps as a result, Colbert was unusually open to the possibility of hiring officials who were not, strictly speaking, qualified by birth, as well as giving Perrault an example of a man of non-noble birth reaching the very highest administrative ranks and noble status. This example was later reflected in his fairy tales, which frequently featured low- and middle-class characters rising into the nobility—a theme rather unusual in the French salon fairy tales.

But even with Colbert leading the way, Perrault's rapid rise to advising Louis XIV on artistic matters and fountains for Versailles, combined with his comparatively low birth and lack of "noble" blood, made Perrault, by the standards of Versailles, a social climber. It also meant that, unlike most of the other French salon fairy-tale writers, he had at least *some* interest in the lower classes.

That interest is reflected in *Little Red Riding Hood,* a story specifically about, as Perrault puts it, "a little country girl." That is, a peasant. A fairly well-off peasant—that, or Perrault had forgotten, or never knew, what starving peasants ate—but still, a peasant. Lacking servants, a mother sends the girl off with a small cake and some butter to check on her grandmother. Along the way, the girl runs into some woodcutters (this is kinda important) and a wolf, who decides not to eat her because of the woodcutters (thus their importance). They have a lovely conversation, because, as Perrault notes, Little Red Riding Hood has never been told not to talk to wolves. The wolf races ahead, tricks his way into the grandmother's home, and consumes her—quickly, since he is starving.

Then he climbs into bed, and waits.

The minute Little Red Riding Hood enters the house, the wolf tells her to put the food down and come into bed with him. She does, removing her clothes first.

In full fairness to the wolf, his specific request was "come get into bed with me," not "strip and *then* come get in bed with me," though possibly, given the hug that follows, Little Red Riding Hood did interpret the wolf's thinking correctly. Or, although the story doesn't mention it, it's possible that Little Red Riding Hood's little detour to gather nuts and chase butterflies left her clothes in the sort of condition that no one, not even a wolf, would want to put on a bed, especially in these pre-laundry machine days. Or maybe Little Red Riding Hood just preferred to go to sleep without her clothes on. Or possibly this was the grandmother's household rule: No sleeping with Grandma until you take off your clothes, a rule I'm pretty sure that we don't want to look at too closely.

Especially since Perrault, at least, had something else in mind, something he made clear in a moral often left out of later editions (including the translation collected by Andrew Lang), but attached to the original version:

> Moral: Children, especially attractive, well bred young ladies, should never talk to strangers, for if they should do so, they may well provide dinner for a wolf. I say, "wolf," but there are various kinds of wolves. There are also those who are charming, quiet, polite, unassuming, complacent, and sweet, who pursue young women at home and in the streets. And unfortunately, it is these gentle wolves who are the most dangerous ones of all. (translation by D. L. Ashliman)

A successful career at court may have left Perrault a defender of royal absolutism, privilege, and Louis XIV, but it had also allowed him to witness the many courtiers who had preyed upon younger women, aristocrats and commoners alike. Some women, admittedly, had been able to use this to their advantage—Francoise d'Aubigne, Marquise de Maintenon, had even managed to marry the king in secret—but others, including those who had dallied, willingly or not, with Louis XIV, had been left ruined or exiled or dead after illicit pregnancies. Others were preyed on for their fortunes. Nor was this behavior, of course, confined to the court of Versailles. It is also likely that Perrault had encountered, in person or through rumor, incidents of child abuse.

In his story, the girl, having willingly entered the wolf's bed, is consumed, with no one showing up to rescue her.

The undressing, and the bed, and the moral have led most commentators to interpret this as a story about the dangers of seduction, but in fairness, I should note that the tale has also been interpreted as a moral lesson about the importance of obeying parents. Little Red Riding Hood, after all, fails to go straight to her grandmother's home, instead deciding to go running after nuts and butterflies, and then ends up dead, but I think this is at best a secondary theme. Perrault's story emphasizes charm, trickery, pursuit—and a wolf waiting in a bed for a young girl to join him.

The story was immensely popular—possibly because the horrifying ending made it the *exact* sort of story that could be told as a terrifying bedroom or fireside story by parents or elder siblings to small, wide-eyed children. (I can neither confirm nor deny at this time doing something of this sort to a younger brother.) Versions appeared in Poland, where the story was later interpreted as an old lunar legend of the wolf swallowing the bright, and sometimes red, moon; in Italy (where the wolf was transformed into an ogre—possibly because several Italian cities, following the example of Republican and Imperial Rome, often portrayed wolves in a more positive light, or possibly because ogres featured in other tales of forbidden or dangerous sexuality); and elsewhere. One French writer, Charles Marelles, dismayed at the unhappy ending, wrote a version of his own, "The True History of Little Golden-Hood," which began with the reassurance that the girl lived, and the wolf died—reassuring to children, if perhaps less reflective of what Perrault had seen at the court of Louis XIV.

The Grimms, however, agreed with Marelles, publishing a version of the story where Little Red Riding Hood and her grandmother are both saved at the last minute by a huntsman who just *happens* to be wandering by and who just *happens* to overhear suspicious snoring, like, um, Huntsman, I mean, yay for knowing just what your neighbors sound like when they snore, but that said, exactly how much time are you spending listening to your neighbors sleep, hmm? And how fortunate that Little Red Riding Hood and her grandmother were swallowed up whole and not, say, chewed, and not particularly damaged from staying inside a wolf's belly and, presumably, digestive juices, other than feeling a bit freaked out about staying in the dark for a bit.

The Grimms also produced a second ending, considerably less well known, where a considerably wiser Little Red Cap, having learned her lesson about wolves, went straight to her grandmother's and locked the door. It ends with the grandmother tricking the wolf into drowning himself in the trough outside her house—at the risk, I might add, of nearly getting little Red Cap eaten up, since she's the one who has to put water into the outside trough in order for the trick to work—but it does work, giving the grandmother more power than she has in other versions of the tale.

Andrew Lang turned down both of the Grimm versions, instead choosing the Perrault version—with Little Red Riding Hood quite, quite dead—for *The Blue Fairy Book* (1889), and the happier Charles Marelles version for *The Red Fairy Book* (1890). But for once, his chosen versions did not become the best known English versions of the tale. Instead, translations of the Grimm version, with its happier ending, were turned into picture books and included in various fairy tale books (it was the one used by the lavishly illustrated fairy tale book I poured over when small), slowly becoming the accepted English version.

Not that *every* American found the tale particularly plausible, particularly American humorist and *The New Yorker* writer James Thurber, whose story "The Little Girl and Wolf," arms Little Red Riding Hood with some common sense and an automatic weapon. It ends, as does Perrault's, with a nice little moral, but a moral that is rather less a caution to young girls and women, and more a reassurance that 20th-century girls were harder to trick.

But Perrault was not worried about the plausibility of his tale: this was a man, after all, that had told stories of pumpkins turning into carriages and cats that could talk and walk in elegant boots and girls who could cough up diamonds and toads. A child's inability to distinguish a grandmother from a wolf was nothing to this, and, in any case, Perrault had seen all too many human wolves and knew all too many grandparents who had not been able to save beloved daughters. His Little Red Riding Hood may not have had a gun, but then again, neither did many of the young girls and women that he had seen at court.

Trickery, Social Climbing, and Possibly Fish: *Puss in Boots*

Some folktale heroes must climb mountains of glass, or reach the ends of the world, or fly upon the back of the West Wind to obtain happiness and good fortune.

Others just need to inherit a cat.

In direct opposition to many fairy tales, which open on a happy note before proceeding directly to disaster, Charles Perrault's *Puss in Boots* opens on disaster: the death of an apparently not very successful miller. I say "apparently not very successful" since, at the end of his life, the miller has little to leave his three sons—one mill, one donkey, and one cat. Since none of these are all *that* easy to divide (although they probably could share in the mill), the sons agree that the oldest son will get the mill, the second son will get the donkey, and the third son just a cat.

This leaves the third son in an inexplicable depression. Yes, inexplicable. I mean, come on, kid. Your oldest brother got the mill, which means he's going to be stuck working there for the rest of his life. Your next brother only got a donkey. But you—you—you got a CAT. The cat currently guarding the most comfortable part of my couch *assures* me that this is the equivalent of inheriting a Faberge egg—and she would certainly know.

Not to mention that this cat *talks*—and not just about the importance of filling her food bowl, or her right to be on pillows designed for humans, or her need for the cat treats that the vet has said she isn't even supposed to be eating. No, this cat talks about the importance of high fashion—boots—before setting out to work. Of a sort.

At this point in the tale, I suspect that many of my fellow cat servants are nodding along, delighted that at least one fairy-tale writer is fully cognizant of the value of cats, while other cat servants are—how to put this—feeling that author Perrault is engaging in *just* a little bit of wish fulfillment about his own cat. Just a little. A feeling that I must confess I share. I don't want to cast aspersions on a cat that, I must assume, was a model of elegance, grace, and beauty, but it does seem possible that Perrault's cat was just perhaps not the sort of cat focused on improving the life of Perrault, but more the sort of cat focused on finding the most comfortable place to take a nap. Which presumably was frequently right on top of whatever manuscripts that Perrault was working on. Or right on Perrault's favorite chair.

No, I am *not* projecting. I merely speak from experience.

Meanwhile, I'm asking, if all of this kid has in the world is this cat, how exactly can this kid afford to buy presumably handmade boots for his cat? Boots elegant enough to trick a king, no less? I'm kinda wondering about this kid here, is what I'm saying.

Anyway, once properly dressed, Puss in Boots—you know, kid, while we're having this conversation, you probably should have named this cat something else, but moving on—begins his elaborate plan to trick the local king into believing that the young miller's son is, in fact, the Marquis de Carabas—a trick that works largely thanks to the size of the French noble class during the time of Louis XIV.

Exact numbers are difficult to calculate, but at least 100,000 people in France at the time could claim *some* sort of noble title—even if many of these titles were simply courtesy titles given to the younger children of nobles. About a century later, this number was estimated to be about 300,000. It was also possible for the very wealthy to, well, not *exactly* purchase titles, but purchase estates associated with titles and then use said titles. Others could and did claim titles from other countries— many perfectly valid, some rather less so. And a few others simply faked their titles completely. France did keep records, but in casual situations—which presumably included such things as a talking cat bringing a gift of dead rabbits—the records were not always checked.

It was thus impossible for the king of France to know every single member of the genuine French nobility, let alone the less genuine—a truth that *Puss in Boots* plays with. Indeed, the rest of the tale echoes the actual methods used by both genuine and considerably less genuine nobles to curry favor with the French court— something presumably witnessed personally by Perrault. The cat delivers lavish gifts of fresh meat, a traditional gift of nobles to the kings; claims that his master just *happens* to be completely naked at the moment thanks to some unfortunate bad luck, perhaps a *little* less traditional; and takes over a castle from its previous landowner (an ogre), in a direct imitation of wealthy French citizens who were purchasing estates to gain titles and better access to the king.

Only one part of the tale rings historically false—the moment when the princess marries the "marquis." Princesses of France were, in general, only allowed to marry other royalty, or enter convents. But even that part of the tale is not, perhaps, all that far-fetched: Perrault had at the very least seen at a distance (and possibly met) Louis XIV's illegitimate daughters, and watched them use their royal blood and wealth to marry noblemen. He may also have known of Louis XIV's secret marriage to a mere marquise.

Thus, for all of its trappings of folklore, *Puss in Boots* is rooted in realism. Like Perrault's *Cinderella*, it serves as an example of the social climbing rampant in the court of Louis XIV and elsewhere in France at the time—something that Perrault, who directly benefited from these opportunities, thoroughly approved of. After all, his two most blatant social climbers—Cinderella and the Marquis de Carabas—end up happily married and rewarded for their efforts.

At the same time, Cinderella earns her happy ending through hard work, patience, courtly skills, and the luck of having a fairy godmother. The Marquis de Carabas, in contrast, does very little except to go along with his cat (showing some sense at last) and charm a lovely princess evidently quite willing to be charmed. Most of the "work"—to use that word lightly—is performed by the cat, and although at first this includes the genuine work of hunting rabbits and bringing them, mostly untouched, to the king, this later is nothing but trickery and lies.

Granted, one of these tricks—gaining the castle of an ogre—does require the cat to speak to an ogre, at considerable risk, and the cat also has to spend considerable time running around to ensure that he stays ahead of the king and the princess, something that unquestionably interfered with his very much needed nap time. But it's hardly the same type of manual labor performed by Cinderella, or, as we'll see later, Donkey-Skin (for different reasons). Rather, it's a focus on deception and verbal trickery.

European folklore, of course, had a long history of talking and trickster animal figures, with cats playing a large role in these tales—presumably thanks to the tendencies of certain cats to, say, knock things off shelves for fun, or, when given the choice of throwing up on easily cleaned tile or not nearly as easily cleaned furniture, choosing the furniture *every. single. time.* Like SERIOUSLY, CAT, WE'VE DISCUSSED THIS so, yes, you ARE DOING THIS ON PURPOSE. In that respect, *Puss in Boots* is simply another part of that tradition.

But in another sense, *Puss in Boots* serves as both warning and comfort. Warning—as a note that not every noble at court was, well, of noble birth, let alone focused on telling the truth. And comfort—giving hope that with a little bit of luck and a lot of cleverness, anyone, even the poor third son of a miller with little to leave, can become a noble someday. After all, a cat is the sort of animal that almost any listener could have the hope of befriending—assuming, of course, that the listener is the sort of person who properly appreciates cats and has access to chicken or fish. (Preferably tuna.)

And, well, even if that cat decides that acquiring the castle of an ogre is just a bit too much work, thanks—well,

I think most cats would agree that mere friendship with a cat is enough to give any human a taste of nobility. In that sense, *Puss in Boots* isn't a fairy tale, but simply truth.

Marie Jeanne L'HERITIER
receüe de l'Académie de Toulouse en 1696.
et de celle de Padove en 1697. fille de M.r
L'heritier Historiographe du Roy née a Paris

Gravé Paris par E. Desrochers rue du Foin prés la rue S.t Jacques

C'est l'Heritiere des Neuf Sœurs
Par sa Prose et sis vers elle charme les Cœurs
Et Minerve avec soin grava dans sa memoire
Tous les traits de la Fable et tous ceux de l'Histoire

Marie-Jeanne L'Heritier de Villandon

Enchantment and Distrust: Marie-Jeanne L'Heritier's *The Discreet Princess*

It perhaps says something that one of the most remarkable aspects of the life of Mademoiselle Marie-Jeanne L'Heritier de Villandon (1664–1734), at least on the surface, was just how *unremarkable* it was. While most of her fellow French salon writers of fairy tales and novels alike were busy conducting scandalous affairs, traveling throughout Europe, dabbling in intrigue, entering and escaping dire marriages, and finding themselves exiled from the court of the none-too-tolerant Louis XIV, and often Paris itself, L'Heritier lived a comparatively quiet and, apparently, chaste life—if one that still had a touch of magic.

The niece of fairy-tale writer Charles Perrault, daughter of a historian, and sister of a poet, she met and befriended several fairy-tale writers in the salons of Paris, and was inspired to write tales of her own. Her talent and erudition eventually earned her a patron, the wealthy Marie d'Orleans-Longueville, Duchess of Nemours, who bequeathed her a small annuity after the Duchess' death. Equally important was a friendship with the formidable and controversial Madeleine de Scudery, these days renowned as the probable writer of *Artamene ou le Grand*

Cyrus, one of the longest novels ever published, but at the time noted for her scholarship and fierce defense of women's education. De Scudery not only befriended the considerably younger woman (De Scudery was born in 1607) but left the fairy tale writer her salon at her death in 1701.

This bequest may have been prompted in part by L'Heritier's *Oeuvres meslees,* a fairy-tale collection published during 1695–1698—the exact same time that her uncle Charles Perrault was publishing his best known tales (*The Sleeping Beauty in the Woods* in 1696, and *Histories ou contes du temps passé*, which included *Sleeping Beauty* again, *Little Red Riding Hood*, *Cinderella,* and *Puss in Boots*).

Indeed, the timing later led some scholars to suspect that Charles Perrault was the actual author of at least some parts of *Oeuvres meslees,* including its best known fairy tale: *The Discreet Princess, or the Adventures of Finette.* The tales do contain some similarities: a rather arch tone, an insistence that they occurred, not in some distant fairy land, but in a very real part of Europe at some point in the past, and comments on the manners of French contemporaries. But *The Discreet Princess* is not only longer and more intricate than most of Perrault's tales, it also contains a rather unusual motif for him: a princess dropping a prince into a sewer.

Also unusually enough for a fairy tale, *The Discreet Princess* is set in a very specific time period—the First Crusade (1095–1099)—though admittedly this is less to make a point about the medieval and Crusader periods, much less provide an accurate description of those times, and more to provide a convenient excuse for sending the king away for a few years—something that the tale emphasizes by noting, just a few sentences later, that "people were quite simple during these happy times," a description that would have startled most of the people involved in the First Crusade. About the only realistic part of this is that the one crusader in the story stays away on crusade for a number of years, fairly typical of many crusaders. Anyway.

The king, hearing about the Crusade, decides to join it, noting only one problem. No, not the cost of the crusade, or the potential issues with leaving his kingdom under the care of ministers, or even the ongoing conflicts that would be sparked by this and later crusades. No, he's worried about his three daughters. Nonchalante is extremely lazy; Babillarde (often called "Babbler" in English translations) *will* not stop talking; and Finette, as befits the youngest of three fairy-tale daughters, is practically perfect in every way, right down to discovering financial cheating by a king's minister. (To repeat: Oh King, why aren't you worried about these ministers, who HAVE been caught attempting to screw you over?)

Despite Finette's cleverness and near perfection and, as the tale will later reveal, a general fondness for her sisters, these are not, the king decides, girls who can be left behind on their own, so, worried about their honor, off he heads to a fairy for some help. The request presumably reflects L'Heritier's Paris experiences, where nobles and others frequently requested assistance from more powerful patrons, but I couldn't help thinking that just maybe the king should have heeded more fairy tales, with their pointed warnings that asking for help from a fairy often lands people in trouble.

The king asks the fairy for three glass distaffs that will magically break when and if any of his daughters lose their honor, which, look, King, I get that you feel your options are limited, but I gotta say: not exactly the most practical choice here. I mean, I get the nod to at least *attempting* to honor what was often seen as women's work, but even I, in the post-industrial age, have seen plenty of women using distaffs, and you know what happens with pretty much all of them? That's right: they fall on the ground. A lot. Making it more than likely that the princesses could be models of excellent deportment and honor and still shatter their distaffs. Though, that said, since distaffs are also generally wrapped with fiber, it's equally possible that the princesses could end up doing something terribly dishonorable and yet find their distaffs left completely whole, protected by the fibers. SPOILER: THAT DOESN'T ACTUALLY HAPPEN but it could, O King, it *could*.

I should note at this point that by "honor," both the king and L'Heritier mean "virginity," not "honesty" or "keeping promises" or "killing lots of Orcs" or "having Brutus explain that really, you are an honorable man" or "standing up for what's right" or any of the sorts of things that we might associate with honor these days. This will be important.

Anyway, perhaps realizing that the glass distaffs are not exactly a foolproof solution, the king also decides to lock the three girls away in a tower, in an echo of the women sent to convents, not always willingly, that L'Heritier had known. Incidentally, at this point even the king admits that none of his daughters have really done anything—other than Finette, who, as it turns out, has managed to infuriate a neighboring prince, Rich-Craft, by uncovering his attempt to deceive their kingdom in a treaty, something Finette's father, with her agreement, responded to by deceiving Rich-Craft in return. The other two are guilty only of laziness and gossip, certainly nothing that would justify imprisonment. But honor is honor, so off the girls head to the tower to be locked up.

Naturally, the two eldest sisters soon become extremely bored, a common fate of princesses locked up in towers in a pre-Netflix age. Equally naturally, Rich-Craft, now out for revenge, decides to take advantage of this. Disguising himself as an old woman, he convinces Babillarde to let him up into the tower. Nonchalante goes along with this in a nonchalant sort of manner. (Look, that's L'Heritier's pun, not mine, so I'm leaving it.) It does not take him too long to shed the disguise and convince first Nonchalante, then Babillarde, to "marry" him (without the benefit of clergy, I should note). Their distaffs shatter. He then turns his attention to Finette, who responds by waving a hammer.

This would convince most men to back away, but not Rich-Craft, who particularly wants revenge on Finette. Thinking fast, Finette carefully makes a bed for "them" on top of a sink with a large drain leading directly to a sewer. She doesn't get on the bed.

Rich-Craft does.

Getting dumped into a sewer does nothing to calm Rich-Craft's temper. After a much needed bath and some time to recover from his wounds, he begins a battle with Finette—who, in the meantime, has fallen into a clinical depression because her sisters have lost their honor, like, Finette, *you just dumped the guy who seduced them into a sewer.* Cheer up. Plus, you have a lot of other things to focus on, like getting kidnapped by Rich-Craft's servants, pushing Rich-Craft into a barrel studded with nails and rolling him down a mountain, sealing your new little nephews into boxes (with air holes, I hasten to add, but still), and disguising yourself as a doctor so you can leave the boxes with Rich-Craft, claiming that the boxes have "medicine" instead of "babies," which you'd think the sounds coming from the boxes would have alerted nearby people to the difference, but maybe these were unusually quiet babies. Or very terrified babies. Whichever. Oh, and welcoming your father home—whose response to all of this is to send his two oldest daughters off to the fairy, who sends them out to do some gardening, which kills them.

No, really. *The Discreet Princess* is *mostly* a warning about the dangers of losing your virginity to any guy who decides to enter your tower dressed as an old woman, but it's *also*, I think, a bit of a jab about aristocrats, or at least French aristocrats, trained to do so little that even pulling weeds kills them. And, admittedly, a hint of the author's lack of interest in either character, once their moral purpose has been met: they're dispatched in two quick sentences.

Finette, you'll be glad to know, ends up happily married to Rich-Craft's brother, Bel-a-Voir, if not before some more Fun Stuff with a sheep's bladder and some blood, which is to say, if you've ever felt that your fairy tales just did not have enough *seriously gross things* like falling into sewers, sheep's bladders, babies sealed into boxes, and blood, this is your kinda tale.

It's also a tale that, for all of its seeming focus on the importance of virginity and honor, primarily focuses on the virtue of *distrust*. With the arguable exceptions of the king and the fairy and some barely-in-the-story fishermen, those who trust others—Nonchalante, Babillarde, Rich-Craft, and Bel-a-Voir—end up suffering greatly for the error of trusting someone's word. Three end up dead; the last loses a brother and has an issue with that sheep's bladder. The fairy sums everything up with her remark, *Distrust is the mother of security.*

The tale also showcases the way seemingly proportional responses to conflict can escalate that conflict—in this case, going from a minor deception involving a treaty, to three dead people and one smushed sheep's bladder and quite a lot of blood. Sure, part of the point here is "lying during treaty negotiations will not, in the long run, go well," but I also can't help but think that it is possible—just barely possible—that had Finette and the king responded to Rich-Craft's initial attempt to deceive them over a treaty by, say, simply declining to sign the treaty, instead of deciding to trick him in return, Rich-Craft might not have decided to come after the three daughters in revenge.

In this, for all its happy ending, *The Discreet Princess* presents a decidedly bleak picture of court life: a life where women can be sent away and locked up on the mere suspicion that they *might* do something; a life where exposing issues in a treaty can later make you a political target; a life where someone *else's* actions might make you a political target; a life where your children can be taken from you (by the good guys) and never seen again; a life where your mother might be killed by gardening. Quite a contrast from the court life presented by L'Heritier's uncle, Charles Perrault, where even commoners like Cinderella and Puss-in-Boot's human could succeed, if only they had the right manners, and, ok, yes, a fairy godmother or a talking cat.

It's probably not a coincidence that the collection was dedicated to Henriette Julie de Castalnau, Countess of Murat (Madame de Murat), banished from Versailles in 1694 for writing political satires. L'Heritier does not offer the options of fairy godmothers or talking cats. Instead, she warns readers to distrust everything, except for self-education. Finette's sisters, who spent their time either in gossip or lazing about, end up dead. Finette, who studied diplomacy, reading, music, and needlepoint, is able to keep herself focused and amused in the tower—and thus able to withstand temptation and survive. It's a powerful argument for the education of women, though it's a bit of a double-edged sword: Finette becomes a target largely because that education and focus brings her into the political side of court life. On the other hand, her less educated sisters aren't spared, becoming targets thanks in part to their family's political manipulations—and end up dead. Finette survives.

I'm left with mixed feelings. On the one hand, the death sentences dealt out to Nonchalante and Babillarde seem overly harsh, to put it mildly. I can quite see that Nonchalante would have been a burden to her servants, but prior to getting locked up in a tower, Babillarde's fondness for gossip hardly seems to have hurt anyone except herself, and, even then, the real wrongdoer here is Rich-craft—who probably wouldn't have succeeded had the princesses *not* been locked in a tower, away from everyone. Babillarde spends time searching for and helping her older sister, and all three of them appear to be genuinely fond of one another. And speaking as a person who has often succumbed to both, the idea that an affinity for laziness and gossip should result in death—well, my skin is crawling a bit over here.

Nor am I all that thrilled that for all of the punishment doled out to Nonchalante, Babillarde, Rich-Craft and Bel-a-Voir, that the other prime mover in all of this—the king—gets away with virtually no consequences whatsoever. Virtually—his two oldest daughters die, but this doesn't seem to bother him very much. Otherwise, his reward for responding to deception with deception, locking his daughters away in a tower and then sending two of them off to their deaths, and marrying off his youngest daughter without consulting or even notifying her? Living happily ever after. Hmm.

And if you're wondering what happened to those little babies in the boxes, well, I am too. About all I can tell you is that the boxes were opened. What happened afterwards? It's a fairy tale, filled with unfairness. I can't reassure you.

But I can say that for all of this, *The Discreet Princess* gives us a fairy-tale princess who isn't afraid to swing a hammer at a foe, drop unworthy princes into a sewer or push them into barrels studded with nails, dress up as a (male) doctor and trick unworthy patients, or use sheep's bladders when necessary. Sure, she also nails babies up in boxes and leaves them with mostly strangers, and sure, she has a tendency to fall into major depressions more than once, but she can still swing that hammer and warn us that princesses might need more than glass slippers to survive court politics. That's something.

Two Visions of Transformation:
Riquet with the Tuft

For the most part, the French salon fairy tale writers all knew each other, at least casually, and all worked from more or less the same sources: oral tales heard in childhood, classical mythology, and collections of Italian fairy tales, in particular Giambattista Basile's *Il Pentameron* and Giovanni Boccaccio's *The Decameron.* So it is not surprising that many of their tales end up sharing some, shall we say, strong similarities, and in some cases nearly identical plots—or even, as with *Beauty and the Beast,* abridgements of another author's original tale. What can be surprising is how and why these tales differ—as a look at two French versions of *Riquet with the Tuft* show.

Catherine Bernard (1662?-1712) worked primarily as a playwright, eventually becoming the most successful woman playwright of her era. She also wrote three novels and multiple poems. None of this earned her much money, however, and she was primarily supported through winning literary prizes and by the patronage of nobles at Louis XIV's court. Although at least one of these patrons seems to have urged her to focus on poetry, her precarious position presumably encouraged her to express herself through fiction rather than the essays, satires, and poems that got many of her fellow writers exiled. Her *Riquet with the Tuft* appears in her third novel, *Ines de Corduve*, published in 1696.

Ines de Corduve features a fairy-tale contest between the eponymous character and a rival—a scene perhaps inspired by similar contests in the salons. Bernard may even have recited *Riquet with the Tuft* at a salon prior to including it in her novel. It's also entirely possible, given her tale's ending, that she never recited it at all prior to including it in her novel. I can't help but think that someone might have suggested one or two changes if she had.

Bernard opens her tale in Grenada—a real place, if one safely outside of France—where a nobleman finds himself with a problem: his beautiful daughter is extremely stupid, enough, Bernard adds, "to make her appearance distasteful." Uh, *ouch.* This is probably one of the cruelest statements about the mentally disabled to appear in French salon fairy tales, though that's partly because, apart from occasional descriptions of characters falling into deep despair, in general, French salon fairy tales tended to avoid the subjects of mental disability and mental health entirely. It's made worse a few sentences later, when it becomes clear that Mama, the beautiful daughter in question, knows that people don't like her very much—but can't figure out why.

By this time it should be fairly clear that this is not necessarily going to be a comforting thing for people with disabilities, mental or physical, to read.

A few sentences later, and Mama runs into a man with a hideous appearance—in Bernard's terms, virtually a monster. Mama wants to flee, but doesn't. The man—Riquet—informs her that they have something in common: he's hideous, which repels people, and she's stupid, which also repels people, but if she wants, he can make her intelligent—if she agrees to marry him within a year. She agrees. Riquet gives her a little rhyme to chant. It works. Very soon she is intelligent, surrounded by lovers—and in love.

Only not with Riquet, and not with someone her parents approve of, either. Arada is good looking, but not wealthy—and, of course, Mama's promised to someone else. Not that her parents know that, but in an aside, they do find themselves rather wishing that Mama had never gained a mind at all and try to warn her about the dangers of love.

At the end of the year, Riquet returns, offering Mama a choice: she can either marry him and become the queen of the gnomes, or she can return to her parents, stripped of her intelligence. She has two days to decide. Two days later, Mama, intelligent enough to know that she will lose Arada if she loses her intelligence, reluctantly agrees to marry him.

This is not *Beauty and the Beast.* The marriage goes badly. Mama despises her husband and, soon enough, contacts Arada, letting him know that she is in the gnome kingdom. Arada comes to her, cheering her up—which immediately rouses the suspicion of Riquet, who changes the conditions: Mama will be intelligent at night—when she is with Riquet—and stupid during the day—when she is with Arada. Mama responds by drugging Riquet. Riquet in turn transforms Arada into a visual double of himself, leaving Mama unable to tell which one is Riquet, and which Arada. Which in turn rather makes me doubt this supposed intelligence Riquet gave her—surely, she could figure out which one was which after a few questions? But apparently not: Mama ends up with two husbands, not knowing which one she can speak to openly. Bernard is not sympathetic:

> But perhaps she hardly lost anything there. In
> the long run, lovers become husbands anyway.

It's an abrupt, brutal, and rather unsatisfactory ending for all three characters—perhaps especially Arada, the complete innocent here, who did nothing more than fall in love with a woman who kinda failed to tell him that she was already engaged to a gnome—a gnome who, moreover, was the only reason she was capable of speaking intelligently. But also for Riquet, who meant well, and ended up trapped in a miserable marriage, judged mostly by his looks, and yes, even for Mama, not always the most sympathetic character here, but who, it seems, wanted to be normal and to fit in—and found herself miserable after choosing to try to be more like other people.

It is perhaps more than pertinent to note here that Bernard herself was born into a Huguenot family and did not convert to Catholicism until 1685, just months before Louis XIV reversed the Edict of Nantes, making the Protestant faith illegal again. (We know the specific date since by the age of 22 or 23, Bernard had made enough of a literary name for herself that her conversion was noted in a French paper.) I'm not *saying* that Bernard converted only to ensure that she could remain at court and write, just that the timing is slightly suspicious. Nor am I suggesting that Bernard wrote highly flattering poems about Louis XIV solely in hopes of getting a pension, just noting that she *did* write highly flattering poems about Louis XIV and did receive a small pension from him. Her defenders, after all, noted that prior to the pension, she had won multiple poetry prizes and was thus a worthy *literary* recipient of this pension. So let us not judge. On the other hand, Bernard's tale suggests that she knew all too well the dangers and stresses of attempting to fit in where you do not fully belong.

Perrault's version, also called *Riquet with the Tuft*, was published a year later—along with *Cinderella, Red Riding Hood*, and other tales—in his *Histories ou contes du temps passe* (1697). It's not entirely clear if Perrault and Bernard were working from the same oral source, or if Perrault simply chose to rewrite Bernard's story, with or without her permission.

What is clear is that he had a very different approach to the tale.

Perrault begins by transforming Riquet from the ugly gnome with powerful magic of Bernard's tale to a very human prince, if one born so ugly that a few people doubt he's human. Luckily, a fairy explains that the little Riquet is so intelligent that he'll be able to charm everyone anyway, despite his looks. It's a bit difficult to figure out how, exactly, she can be so sure about this, given that he's just a squalling newborn when she makes this pronouncement, but, fairies. In any case, her prediction turns out to be completely true, possibly echoing Perrault's own experiences at Versailles, where, based on various portraits, a number of downright hideous people managed to overcome that particular issue and become powerful, influential, and even popular.

It would perhaps miss the point entirely if I noted that many of those people had money or powerful relatives.

Anyway.

Riquet also receives a powerful gift: whomever he chooses to love will seem equally intelligent, just because he's in love.

Meanwhile, over in the next kingdom, the royal family is dealing with one beautiful but stupid daughter, and one ugly but intelligent daughter. The dismayed family turns to a fairy for help, who notes that she can't do much about the looks, but will give the beautiful daughter one gift: whomever she chooses to love will seem beautiful just because she's in love.

You can probably guess, at this point, where this story is going—indeed, the main advantage Bernard's tale has over Perrault's is that her story is considerably less predictable, even if Perrault's story is more charming, comforting, and, well, a lot more fun—partly thanks to its much happier ending. The beautiful princess finds herself incredibly jealous of her ugly but more popular sister, to the point of feeling that she would willingly give up all of her beauty for half of her sister's intelligence. Fortunately enough, for all of Riquet's supposed intelligence, he turns out to be remarkably fixated on looks, falling in love with the beautiful princess based on her portraits alone. When, after arriving at her kingdom, he finds her melancholy, he is surprised. When she explains that her unhappiness stems from her lack of intelligence, he notes:

> There's no greater proof of intelligence, madam, than the belief that we do not have any. It

is the nature of the gift that the more we have,
the more we believe we are deficient in it.

I sense a slight—a *very* slight—slam at some of his
fellow courtiers here, though neither Riquet nor Perrault
are rude enough to name names. In any case, the princess
is not intelligent enough to be convinced by this, so, as
in Bernard's tale, Riquet offers to make her intelligent—
if she'll agree to marry him within a year. The princess
agrees. She returns to her court, dazzling everyone with
her new wit—including a rather handsome prince that
she can't help being more than a bit into. Her parents approve, assuring her—in direct contradiction to the more
usual situation with nobility and royalty—that she can
choose a husband for herself.

One year later, a far more thoughtful princess meets
Riquet out in the gardens. She notes that she was un-
certain about marrying him back when she lacked intelligence; does he *really* want to marry her now that she's
more intelligent—and thus, harder to please? He asks if
she has any other issues with him beyond his appearance.
She assures him that she doesn't. He points out that she
has the power to make anyone she falls in love with handsome with a single wish. She makes the wish. And with
that, they live happily ever after, intelligently and beautifully, although Perrault points out that *some* people—not
naming names, you understand—claim that this was less
magic, and more love, which transformed all of Riquet's
flaws to heroic, handsome points in his favor.

I concede the possibility, but I also have to note the
difference between the two tales: Bernard, who never
married, and remained on the outside of the French

court, and who converted from the religion of her home to the established religion of her court, not only presents a woman who, for all her intelligence, is unable to see beyond appearances, but also leaves us with a deeply unhappy marriage. Perrault, who enjoyed an extremely successful, social-climbing career at court, assures us that true love can allow us—or, at least princesses—to see beyond initial appearances, and fall in love with people who may appall us on a purely superficial level. One of them, I think, would have believed the story of *Beauty and the Beast.* The other would not.

Catherine Bernard stopped publishing in 1698, reportedly turning to prayer and the study of religion instead, with the royal pension providing just enough to live on, to save her the necessity of publishing. She died fourteen years later, in 1712. Twenty years after her death, her work became the subject of a major and nasty literary fight, where some critics, mostly friends of Voltaire, claimed that Bernard's two plays, *Laodamie, reine d'Epire* (1689) and *Brutus* (1690), had actually been written by her (probable) cousin Fontenelle, as other critics, mostly enemies of Voltaire, claimed that Voltaire had copied various passages of Bernard's *Brutus*—and that Bernard's play was better. An infuriated Voltaire announced that most of Bernard's *Brutus* had absolutely, positively been written by her cousin, and was not very good anyway, stirring up the fight all over again. For a time, Bernard was better known as a subject of this controversy rather than for her own work or for her fairy tales, until the 1980s when she once again became a subject of academic research.

It might have comforted her to know that Perrault's version of her tale followed her into obscurity. Even in its initial publication, the tale never achieved the same popularity as *Cinderella* or *Puss in Boots,* or even his disturbing *Donkey-Skin.* It was translated with his other tales into English, but for whatever reason, English readers also failed to warm to the tale. Andrew Lang, who happily included Perrault's other tales in his collections, including *Donkey-Skin*, left this one out.

It's rather a pity: ugliness is so often associated with wickedness in fairy tales that it's refreshing to see it depicted here as something that can be associated with good, in tales where beauty, for once, is not regarded either as a hallmark of goodness or even as something particularly desirable, and where intelligence is worth sacrificing almost everything for—even the chance of future happiness.

Henriette Julie de Murat

Imprisonment and the Fairy Tales of Henriette Julie de Murat

Most of the French salon fairy-tale writers lived lives mired in scandal and intrigue. Few, however, were quite as scandalous as Henriette Julie de Murat (1670?–1716), who, contemporaries whispered, was a lover of women, and who, authorities insisted, needed to spend some quality time in prison, and who, she herself insisted, needed to dress up as a man in order to escape said prison—and this is before I mention all of the rumors of her teenage affairs in Brittany, or the tales of how she more than once wore *peasant clothing* in the very halls of Versailles itself.

Oh, and she also wrote fairy tales.

Partly because her life was mired in scandals that she, her friends, and family members wanted to suppress, and partly because many documents that could have clarified information about her life were destroyed in the French Revolution and World War II, not all that much is known about Madame de Murat, as she was generally known. Most sources, however, seem to agree that Henriette Julie de Castelnau Murat was born in Brest, Brittany, in 1670, and was the daughter of a marquis. I say "most sources" since some scholars have argued that Murat was actually born in the Limousin (now Nouvelle-Aquitaine) area, and a few more recent studies have claimed that she was actually born in Paris in 1668, and no one seems completely certain about the marquis part, although she was born into the aristocracy.

Records about her later life are often equally contradictory, when not, apparently, outright fabricated. For instance, something seems to be just a touch off with one of the more famous stories about her, apparently first told in 1818, a century after her death, by the respectable lawyer Daniel Nicolas Miorcec de Kerdanet. According to this tale, shortly after her presentation at court and marriage, she impressed (according to some accounts) or scandalized (according to more prim accounts) Queen Maria Theresa of Spain, Louis XIV's first wife, by wearing peasant clothing from Brittany in the royal presence. (You can all take a moment to gasp now.) Reported by numerous fairy-tale scholars, the anecdote certainly fits with the rest of the scandalous stories told about her life, but, assuming that Murat was born in 1670 (as most of the people repeating the anecdote claim) and married at the age of 16 (as suggested by other documents), the earliest date for this scandal would have been sometime in 1686—three years after Maria Theresa's death in 1683.

It is of course very possible that Miorcec de Kerdanet confused Maria Theresa with Madame de Maintenon, Louis XIV's second, considerably less publicized wife, but nonetheless, this sort of easily checked error does not entirely inspire confidence in other tales about her—including his report that Murat had already enjoyed several wildly romantic (read: sexual) relationships before her arrival in Versailles at the age of 16. I'm not saying she *didn't*. I'm just saying that in this case, the respectable lawyer doesn't strike me as the most trustworthy source.

It's also possible that Murat was, indeed, born in 1668, making it just barely possible that she was presented at court in 1683, at the age of 15—just in time to scandalize Maria Theresa on her deathbed.

Which is to say, feel free to treat pretty much *everything* you read in the next few paragraphs with some degree of skepticism.

We are, however, fairly certain that Madame de Murat spent her childhood in either Brittany, Limousin, or Paris, or all three, possibly making one or two trips to Italy, or possibly never visiting Italy or even leaving France, at all. We think that, as the daughter of a marquis, she was officially presented at the court of Versailles at some point—perhaps when she was sixteen, ready to be married, or perhaps when she was twenty, or perhaps somewhere in between this. At some point after this presentation—either in 1686 (if we believe that respectable attorney Miorcec de Kerdanet again) or in 1691 (if we believe some more recent French scholarship), Murat married Nicolas de Murat, Comte de Gilbertez. Soon afterwards, she seems to have started attending the French literary salons, where she met various fairy-tale writers, including Madame d'Aulnoy, Marie-Jeanne L'Heritier, and Catherine Bernard. Perhaps with their encouragement, or perhaps not, she began to write poems and enter literary competitions.

In 1697, she published a bestseller—*Mémoires de Madame la Comtesse de M*****. The work was apparently intended less as a factual account of her marriage and more as a response to *Mémoires de la vie du comte D**** avant sa retraite,* by Charles de Marguetel de Saint-Denis, seigneur de Saint-Evremond, a popular work which had appeared the year before—apparently without his authorization—and which depicted women as deceitful and incapable of living a virtuous life. (I should note that many objective observers said similar things about Saint-Evremond.) Madame de Murat's own life may not have exactly been a paradigm of virtue by French standards up until that point—although the worst was yet to come—, but she could not let these accusations stand. From her viewpoint, women were generally the victims of misfortune and gossip, not perpetrators—even as she also blamed women for starting gossip, rather than working together in solidarity and mutual support. It was the first of many of her works to emphasize the importance of friendship between women.

The heroine of the memoir finds herself subject to emotional and physical abuse early in her marriage after an innocent visit from a former suitor—perhaps one of those alleged relationships back in Brittany. After fleeing her husband, she was urged by family members, including her father, to return to him. How much of this reflected Murat's own experience is difficult to say. The available records suggest that her father died when she was very young, casting doubt upon that part of the tale, but other records and stories do suggest that Murat's marriage was unhappy at best, and possibly abusive at worse. I could not find any record of her husband's response to these accusations.

Presumably encouraged by her popular success, Murat turned to fairy tales, writing several collections as a direct response to Perrault's *Histories ou contes du temps passé*—the collection that brought us the familiar *Puss in Boots, Cinderella, Little Red Riding Hood,* and *Sleeping*

Beauty, as well as the critical response to these tales. As someone who delighted in fairy tales, Madame de Murat did not object to their subject matter, but she did object to Perrault and various literary critics claiming that fairy tales were best suited for children and servants—mostly because that claim dismissed all of the careful, intricate work of the French salon fairy-tale writers, many of them her friends. From de Murat's point of view, she and her friends were following in the rich literary tradition of Straparola and other Italian literary figures, as well as helping to develop the literary form of the novel—not writing mere works for children. Even if some of the French fairy-tale writers *were* writing works for children. As proof of her own intellectual accomplishments, she joined the Accademia dei Riccovrati of Padua—a group with a certain appreciation of the Italian literary tradition.

She also found herself embroiled in increasingly serious scandals at Versailles. By some accounts, she was first banished from court in 1694, after publishing the political satire *Historie de la courtisanne.* In 1699, a high-ranking police officer of Paris, Rene d'Argenson, claimed that she was a lover of women, forcing Murat to flee Paris—and leave her husband—for some time. Two years later, she was discovered to be pregnant, which did nothing to convince anyone of her virtue. In 1702, she was exiled to the Chateau de Loches, at some distance from Paris.

All this *should* have been scandalous enough—but Murat added to it with a daring attempt to escape from the chateau, dressed as a man. Alas, her plan failed, and she was sent to various prisons before her return to the more pleasant confinement of the Chateau de Loches in 1706.

The Chateau de Loches may have been an improvement from her previous prisons, but Madame de Murat found exile intensely boring. To combat her boredom, she hosted late night gatherings which, depending upon whom you choose to believe, were either nights of debauchery and even orgies (whee!), or attempts to recreate the Paris salons she so missed, dedicated to witty conversation and fairy tales in this small chateau/half-prison and town far from Paris. Or both. These parties could not have been exactly cheap, and exactly how she financed any of this remains unclear—but Murat decided that the parties should continue, and so they did.

When not hosting parties, she continued to write fairy tales and experimental novels, and—according to legends—further scandalized the locals by wearing red clothing to church. She was not allowed to return to Versailles and Paris until after Louis XIV's death in 1715.

Sadly for those hoping for further scandal, Murat died shortly afterwards, in 1716.

Murat unabashedly admitted to plagiarizing ideas for many of her works—though that confession was also meant in part to inform her readers that she had, indeed, read Straparola and other literary figures and thus should be considered a *literary* writer. She noted that other women, too, drew from Straparola—granting them this same literary authority—but at the same time, insisted that *her* adaptations had nothing to do with *theirs:* she worked alone. Thus, she managed to claim both literary authority *and* creativity. She may also have hoped that this claimed literary authority would encourage readers to overlook the more scandalous stories of her sleeping with women, cross-dressing, and wearing inappropriate clothing to church.

In some cases, she outright incorporated the works of her fellow fairy-tale writers, seemingly with their permission. Her novel *A Trip to the Country,* for instance, contains material definitely written by Catherine Bedacier Durand (1670–1736), and she continued to exchange tales with other fairy-tale writers. This can make it difficult to know for certain which stories are absolutely, positively, definitely hers—Marina Warner, for one, prudently decided to say that one tale, *Bearskin*, was just "attributed to" Henriette-Julie de Murat. For the most part, however, tales firmly associated with Murat tend to be intricate, containing tales within tales, and often combine classical mythology with French motifs, allowing us to make some tentative identifications.

A fairly typical example is "The Palace of Revenge," found in her collection *Les nouveaux contes des fees*, published in 1698—that is, four years after her possible first banishment from court, but shortly before her later imprisonment. It is a darkly cynical tale of love and fairies and stalking, containing within it another tale of possessive, forbidden love, one that—unlike the popular conception of fairy tales, starts happily and ends, well, a little less so.

As it begins, a king and queen of Iceland have a beautiful daughter named Imis and a nephew, conveniently provided by Cupid, named Philax. Equally conveniently, the daughter and nephew fall in love and find complete happiness—in the first three paragraphs.

This is about when things go wrong, what with unclear oracles (perhaps an echo of the vague fortunes told by questionable fortunetellers), not overly helpful fairies, enchanted trees that once were princes, and a small man named Pagan, who turns out to be a powerful enchanter. Pagan, convinced that he is far more in love and better suited to Imis than Philax is, begins to pursue her. Imis initially fails to take this seriously, convinced that her contempt for Pagan and obvious love for Philax will make Pagan retreat. The enchanter does not. Instead, Pagan transports Philax to a gloomy forest and brings Imis to his palace, showering her with gifts and entertainment. The enchanted palace is somewhat like the one in *Beauty and the Beast*—but Imis is unmoved.

What does move her: finally seeing Philax again—happily throwing himself at the feet of another woman, a lovely nymph. As it happens, this is all perfectly innocent—Philax is throwing himself at the feet of the nymph out of gratitude, not love, but it looks bad, and Imis understandably assumes the worst. Nonetheless, even convinced of his infidelity, Imis decides to stay with Philax. Pagan takes his revenge by imprisoning them in a delightful enchanted castle—telling them that they will remain their forever.

A few years later, both are trying desperately—and unsuccessfully—to destroy the palace.

A story within the story tells of a fairy who, rather than showering gifts on reluctant suitors, enchanted them—and after they broke her enchantment, transformed them into trees. And trees they remain, if trees able to remember their lives as princes. Philax never tries to save them,

Murat would have, and did, sympathize with all of this: having her innocent actions spun into scandal, imprisonment in castles (if less enchanted and delightful than the ones she describes), and an inability to change at least some of those trapped by the more powerful—including herself. She knew of people like Pagan, unable to take no for an answer, and did not blame their victims—even as she recognized that those people might take their revenge. And she knew about magic. Thus her fairy tales: cynical, pointed, and not entirely able to believe in happy endings.

I've Fallen for *Who* Now?
The French fairy tale of *Bearskin*

We're all fairly familiar with the tale of the girl who meets her prince at a ball. But what if the princess just happens to already be legally and religiously married—to an ogre? And is having just a *few* issues with her current personal appearance, by which I mean "sometimes she looks like a bear, although the sort of bear that collects flowers in the wood, not the sort of bear that eats people, although frankly, given the sort of story she's in, she probably *should* be eating more people."

You'd have the French salon fairy tale, *Bearskin*.

Bearskin is generally attributed to Henriette-Julie de Murat, largely because it appeared in a revised edition of Murat's last novel, *Les lutins du Château de Kernosy* (*The Sprites of Kernosy Castle*). Since the fairy tale did not appear in the original edition of the novel, however, some scholars believe that the story was actually written by Marie-Madeleine de Lubert, who had prepared the revised edition. Other scholars believe that Lubert restored a story that was in the original manuscript but was removed by the novel's first publishers most probably because of Murat's own scandalous past episodes of dressing up like a peasant (gasp) and a man (shock). A story about dressing up in bearskins, while fitting in perfectly here, was hardly the sort of tale designed to help people forget the worst scandals of Madame de Murat— a discretion her publishers may have assumed was necessary in order to sell the novel and ensure that Madame de Murat could continue to pay for her fabulous parties. So, it's possible that Lubert merely wanted to restore the original text.

On the other hand, Lubert was also a writer of fairy tales. Unlike Murat, Lubert lived a comparatively scandal-free life—at least publicly; if she did sleep with women or wear male clothing or escape from prisons, she did so discreetly. This in turn means we know considerably less about her life—even the year of her death can be only guessed at. We do know that she decided to focus on writing, and that marriage would be an obstacle to that goal. She apparently corresponded at some length with several major French authors of the period, including Voltaire, but most of this correspondence seems to have been lost, possibly during the French Revolution.

What we also know is that Lubert chose to publish many of her fairy tales anonymously—and sneaking one of her own stories into a Murat novel was *just* the way to get her work published without admitting that she'd actually written it. If, then, anyone objected to what turned out to be a rather significant, even startling, amount of bestiality, she could blame the scandalous Murat. If no one did, she could—modestly enough—admit to trusted friends that this tale was hers.

So this could be her tale. Like other tales associated with or identified as written by Lubert, *Bearskin* has a happy ending—quite unlike many of the more ambiguous or cynical or both endings associated with Murat's fairy tales. And, like Lubert's tale of *Princess Camion*, *Bearskin* is very very insistent that it's all *perfectly all right* to feel physically attracted to and even fall in love with an animal—as long as that animal is charming, of course. It's an insistence that no other French salon fairy-tale writer felt like making, particularly to that extent—including fairy-tale writers who eventually paired up their lovely princes and princesses with beasts. Enchanted beasts, but still. Indeed, Gabrielle-Suzanne Barbot de Villeneuve and Jeanne-Marie Leprince de Beaumont both went well out of their way to assure readers that Beauty did not find the Beast at all physically attractive. *Bearskin* takes a different approach, one not particularly associated with Murat's other tales.

Bearskin emphasizes the importance of women supporting one another, a theme that frequently appears in Murat's novels—but the friendship between the girls in the tale is a bit truncated and not all *that* supportive. And as a final note, *Bearskin* is somewhat less narratively complex than some of Murat's other works—by which I mean that it has only one story, not stories nestled within stories—and avoids using classical motifs, which Murat used liberally in other works. Then again, writers don't *always* write within the same vein. Which is to say, *Bearskin* could be by Murat, or could be by Lubert. Or perhaps was started by Murat and ended by Lubert. Since my French is not *exactly* up to analyzing stylistic and literary differences, let's just follow Marina Warner here and go with "attributed to Murat."

Bearskin has much in common with Perrault's *Donkey-Skin* (a tale we'll be getting to) and various versions of *Beauty and the Beast*, as well as Perrault's version of *Sleeping Beauty*, showcasing how the French salon fairy-tale authors could mix the same elements to come up with distinct tales, but also, another reminder that the French salon fairy-tale authors read and listened to one another's works, only rarely writing with full independence.

It starts, in typical fairy-tale fashion with the birth of the young princess Hawthorn, who is, also in typical fairy-tale fashion, beautiful and charming. But almost immediately, *Bearskin* strikes another note not found in the similar opening to Perrault's *Sleeping Beauty*: The princess is an only child, yes, but not because her parents had not been able to have other children. Her brothers all died young. An echo, certainly, of real-world situations among royals and nobles alike; only one of Louis XIV's legitimate children survived to adulthood. The tale also makes a point of noting that her royal parents had the princess carefully educated—something that helps her later survival. Murat and Lubert both championed the education of women.

And in another switch from other fairy tales, the princess is not exactly eager to find her prince—a hesitation her parents support. Alas, King Rhinoceros, an ogre, hears about her beauty and sends an ambassador—also an ogre—to warn the court that if she does not come to him to be his bride, he will send an army of ogres to eat the entire kingdom.

Somewhat reminiscent of a similar choice in *Beauty and the Beast*, but switched: in that tale, Beauty faced only the loss of her father, but more than willingly took his place—after his protests. In this tale, the princess initially protests—but eventually agrees to wed the ogre. In another echo of real-world events, she is married to the ogre by proxy, with his ambassador taking his place at the altar—a ceremony recognized by canon law at the time and commonly practiced with royal marriages.

Hawthorn sets off to the kingdom of the ogres—but not alone. A friend, Corianda, travels with her. Corianda turns out to be the sort of friend who heads off to talk to your fairy godmother behind your back, and then fails to tell you that your fairy godmother is really *really* ticked off, which seems to me to be the sort of thing that's *kinda* important to know in fairy tales. I mean, pause for a moment: what would have happened to Cinderella if *her* godmother had been ticked off? Well. Some of those mice and rats would have had a much less exciting evening, at the least. And I can't even excuse this by saying that Corianda isn't aware that they are in a fairy tale—after all, not only are the two of them journeying off to the kingdom of the ogres, but one of them has a fairy godmother that the other one is gossiping with. Chat with people, Corianda, is all I'm saying.

Anyway, once at the kingdom of the ogres, Princess Hawthorn decides that she just can't possibly go through with it, even if she doesn't have a fairy godmother. Corianda, thinking quickly, decides that the best way to proceed is to sew Hawthorn up into some bearskins that the ogre just happens to have lying around—he likes hunting bears, apparently, and hasn't bothered to hire magical servants to put the bearskins away in their proper place. It's not a bad idea—until Hawthorn turns into an actual bear. The one benefit here: in bear form, Hawthorn is able to escape to another kingdom. The huge freaking bad point: SHE LEAVES CORIANDA BEHIND WITH THE OGRE.

So much for friendship, guys. I mean, sure, Corianda didn't exactly keep Hawthorn clued into all of the fairy gossip, but she did *sew the princess into a bear*, well enough to transform the girl, which I feel Hawthorn deeply underappreciated.

Anyway. Still a bear, Hawthorn ends up in the Kingdom of Felicity, which just happens to be ruled by a guy who likes to hunt things like bears. This could be awkward, especially given that Hawthorn can't speak, but luckily she has the good sense to bow before the king, clueing him into the fact that she's not exactly the ordinary sort of bear. A few sentences later, and we have this:

> Overcome with joy to discover that she was capable of reason, the king kissed her.

….did I say *could* be awkward? Let's go to VERY DEFINITELY AWKWARD, since Hawthorn is still—THIS IS VERY IMPORTANT—A BEAR. AND NOT A TALKING BEAR, EITHER.

The kiss does not, as you might expect, transform the bear back into a human, but it *does* make the bear jump back. There's more confusion, kinda solved by orange branches, really, and the king decides to create an elaborate grotto for her to live in with nice statues. I would have thought that honey would be a more appropriate gift, but perhaps I just have *Winnie the Pooh* on my mind. Moving on. The king visits the bear, like, a lot. I mean, like a suspicious amount of a lot. Like this:

> He came to see her at every possible moment, and brought her into every conversation: he was crazy about her.

Most bears would have figured things out by now. Hawthorn, a more humble sort of bear, instead thinks:

The delectable Zelindor had awoken her feelings, but how could he find her attractive in
this frightful shape?

I dunno, Hawthorn. He's *already kissed you.* He's
built you a grotto. I can understand you *not* wanting to
believe that the guy you're falling for is deeply into bears,
but the clues here are kinda obvious.

Instead of thinking things through, Hawthorn responds by carving terrible poetry on trees. We've all been
there. The tale, I should note, calls these "the prettiest
verses imaginable" but (a) most French salon fairy tales
are somewhat prone to exaggeration, and (b) princesses
transformed into bears unable to realize that when a king
builds a grotto for you after kissing you this MEANS
HE LIKES YOU can hardly be expected to write great
poetry. Suddenly, a fish leaps out.

Said fish turns out to be the fairy Medlar, who hand-
waves away the entire "legally married to an ogre" thing
(I'm not *entirely* sure of the grounds for this, but I expect that transforming into a bear is grounds for annulment in most legal systems) and allows Hawthorn to
stop being a bear at night. Hawthorn responds to this by
writing more bad poetry and plucking flowers to leave
at the king's door. If any of you are thinking, but WAIT,
what happened to the friend, well, I was thinking that
too, but this story needs to rush on to the king rethink-
ing his sexuality:

> For his part, the young king, as he reflected
> how clever the bear was, dared not admit to
> himself that he found her irresistibly attractive.

Uh huh.

I am happy to tell you that this all does—*eventually*—work out without *too* much overt bestiality, within the highly proper bounds of a second marriage, this one not by proxy, and a little less happy to tell you that in a moment reminiscent of the end of Perrault's *Sleeping Beauty*, the ogre, for one, is not exactly in favor of this annulment, and responds by trying to kill the young children of the bear—er, the princess—and the king, framing their murders to look like the work of the bear—er, princess. At this point, although the princess is now back in human form, the king falls out of love with her.

Uh *huh*.

At this point, whoever wrote the story decided—or realized—that everyone in the story had gone through quite enough, and everyone not in the story would quite possibly be starting to ask a few questions about the writer and bears, and hastily created a not overly satisfactory, but happy enough ending.

The stuff about bears aside, *Bearskin* is another fascinating meditation on the roles of women in the aristocracy, mirroring the real-life concerns of many aristocratic women: arranged marriages with strange husbands, slanderous accusations that could lead to exile and imprisonment (in the case of Madame de Murat) or even death, the critical importance of friendship, and the deaths of far too young children. And, oh, yes, admitting that sometimes—just sometimes—you can find yourself attracted to the most inappropriate people. Or bears.

Jeanne-Marie Leprince de Beaumont

The Dangers of Propaganda, Flattery, and Violence Toward Cats:
Prince Desir and Princess Mignone

Jeanne-Marie Leprince de Beaumont is best known to English readers for her compact retelling of *Beauty and the Beast*, which, with a few small edits from Andrew Lang, became the best known version of that tale, and more recently, the basis for a film that brought in more than one billion dollars at the box office even though Angela Lansbury failed to appear in it.

But Madame de Beaumont—frequently desperate for cash—did not content herself with writing just one fairy tale. She wrote seventy books, including *Le Magasin des Enfants* (1756), a collection of didactic fairy tales aimed at older children. In *Beauty and the Beast*, she stressed the need for girls to distinguish between appearances and reality. In another tale in the collection, *Prince Desir and Princess Mignone*, she took another look at this theme—this time, warning against the dangers of flattery and self-deception.

It all starts with an attempt to harm a cat.

No, really. As the story starts, a king has fallen in love with a beautiful princess, as fairy-tale kings do when they are not sending out their sons on impossible magical quests or imprisoning their daughters in towers. Only one problem: the princess is under a spell and can only be released if someone steps on the tail of her cat.

I am sorry to say that the king leaps to this challenge. I can only assume that he (a) dislikes cats, and (b) doesn't know all that much about cats. The cat, like any proper cat, is not at all thrilled by the idea of a mere *human* stepping on his tail, and easily evades the king for a week. That is, until finally the king manages to find the cat asleep. And he doesn't just step on the cat's tail, he STOMPS on it.

The cat, naturally, is beyond furious about this. A little less naturally, the cat—who turns out to be an evil sorcerer in disguise, and let me just say, I approve of his choice to spend his life focusing on cat naps and tuna instead of evil magic, not to mention his choice to force the enchanted princess to adopt him instead of marrying him—decides to curse not the king, but the king's son. I may have to rethink my previous kind thoughts about this cat sorcerer. After all, the king's *son* hasn't stepped on any cat tails. (Yet.) In any case, the cat sorcerer announces that the king's son will never be happy until he finds out that his nose is too long, and if the king even mentions this, well, the king will die.

I'm even more sorry to say that the king's response to this is to laugh. King! This guy isn't just an evil sorcerer. He's a DIGNIFIED CAT WHOSE TAIL YOU STOMPED ON. SHOW SOME RESPECT. On the other hand, it's probably safe to assume that as a fairy-tale king, this guy has heard much more dire threats in his time: "Your kid will have a long nose" is a lot less dire than, say, "your daughter will die after touching a spinning wheel."

In due course, the king and his new wife have a son, Prince Desir. The story does not tell us if they also have a cat. I like to think that they had a few arguments about this, and the annoyed sorcerer just sent another cat, who, being a cat, decided to stay whether or not they wanted him. But I digress. The son, as cursed, has an enormous, enormous nose. Given that the curse *specifically states* that the kid will be unhappy until he finds out that his nose is too long, you would think that both parents would go to extreme efforts to let the kid know this as early as possible. Say when he's three. Then again, the king can't tell anyone about the curse, and the queen has decided to listen to comforting courtiers, who assure her that her son's nose isn't overly long, it's just *Roman.*

And soon, this becomes the approach of the entire court: to lie to the Queen and her son. Only long-nosed people are allowed anywhere near Desir. He is told dreadful tales about people with short noses and assured that all great leaders and beautiful princesses had long, long noses. The various courtiers go to great lengths to lengthen their own noses, and his room is filled with pictures of long-nosed people. Desir grows up believing that his giant nose is a mark of beauty and distinction.

This is all very kind and reassuring, no doubt, and at least ensures that Desir won't grow up with major self-confidence issues—kinda big for a potential king. But at the same time, it also means that Desir grows up believing a complete lie—and also grows up with no awareness of how those outside the court might view him or mock him.

Which becomes an immediate problem when Desir falls in love with the portrait of Mignone, a beautiful princess—a princess with a little upturned nose. A nose that Desir's courtiers, now trained for twenty years to mock, quite understandably *do* mock—only to find themselves banished from the court as a result. Another courtier hastily adds that noses are *completely different* for women, plus, Cleopatra apparently had a tip-tilted nose; this nice bit of wisdom and fake history gains the courtier a nice monetary award.

Meanwhile, Desir heads off to meet the princess, who is immediately captured by the sorcerer, apparently still sore about the whole cat tail thing. (I feel certain that all of my readers who have been honored with the friendship of cats or, failing that, honored with the presence of cats who have graciously agreed to adorn their homes, can understand this.) Off Desir heads to find her, only to run into an elderly fairy who laughs at his nose. He laughs at hers. They have a long and increasingly tense conversation about noses before Desir stalks off, wondering why everyone keeps bringing up his nose.

The fairy, deciding that it's about time to get to the end of the story, captures Princess Mignone and places her into a crystal palace—where Desir can see her, but not kiss her, because, well, the nose. And with that truth finally admitted, his nose shrinks down to normal size, he and the princess live happily ever after, and Beaumont has just enough time to sneak in a nice moral about how self-love can keep us from seeing important truths about ourselves.

Which—okay, as said, a nice moral, but in this case, Desir seems to be suffering not so much from misguided self-love, as brainwashing. He's been trained to think that his large nose is delightful. His problem is not so much failing to see his own flaw as being unable to break out of years of conditioning. And his *real* problem is that so many courtiers were so desperate to flatter him that they created an alternative reality based on falsehoods.

Which makes this a story not just about self-deception, but about the evils of flattery—and the dangers of listening to only one viewpoint.

Andrew Lang included the tale in *The Blue Fairy Book* (1889), thus including it with the famous tales of *Cinderella*, *Sleeping Beauty*, *Puss in Boots*, *Hansel and Gretel*, *Little Red Riding Hood*, and *Beauty and the Beast*. As he had with Beaumont's *Beauty and the Beast*, Lang made a few changes to the tale. Prince Desir, for instance, became the more child-friendly Prince Hyacinth, and Princess Mignone became the Dear Little Princess, which—ok, it's a fair enough translation, but it still feels like depriving her of a name. The moral at the end of the story was tucked into the fairy's final speech, making it feel a little less like a tacked-on moral and a little more like part of the tale. For the most part, however, Lang stayed close to the original version, making fewer changes than he had to *Beauty and the Beast*—perhaps out of admiration for the original. And as if to emphasize its importance, Lang placed the tale second in the collection—before such tales as *Cinderella*, *Beauty and the Beast*, and *Little Red Riding Hood*.

And yet, for whatever reason, "Prince Hyacinth and the Dear Little Princess" never seemed to enter the public consciousness in the same way as these other tales have. Children and parents not liking the idea that stepping on a cat could remove a spell? The lack of danger in the rest of the tale? Its focus on gentle sarcasm instead of magic? Or its illustration of how easy it can be for children, and even clever adults, to believe in constructed realities and lies? How easy it is to make someone believe something objectively untrue—and how difficult it can be to break free from those beliefs, even when encountering other opinions?

I don't know. I only know that as an illustration of the power and dangers of conditioning and propaganda, *Prince Desir/Prince Hyacinth and Princess Mignone/the Dear Little Princess*, if lacking some of the terror and trauma of other, better known fairy tales, still resonates today.

*Anne Claude Philippe de Tubières-Grimoard de Pastels
de Lévis, comte de Caylus*

Fairy Tales in Conversation:
Princess Minute and King Floridor
by the Comte de Caylus

Anne Claude Philippe de Tubières-Grimoard de Pastels de Lévis, comte de Caylus, marquis d'Esternay, baron de Branscac (1692–1765), generally known by the considerably shorter name of Comte de Caylus, not only had the enviable honor of having about the longest name yet of anyone discussed in this book, but also of being the grandson of a first cousin of Madame de Maintenon, the second, secret wife of Louis XIV. This in turn ensured that he and his mother had access to the very cream of French society—and the French salons, where fairy tales still remained a prime source of amusement.

Caylus flourished in this atmosphere. After fighting in the War of the Spanish Succession from 1709 to 1714, an experience that gave him a permanent aversion to war, he chose to travel through Europe, eventually making his way to Italy, Greece, and the Ottoman Empire. Here, he fell in love with antiquities and archaeology, even joining the dig at Herculaneum, where the wealthy Emmanuel Maurice de Lorraine, Duke of Elbeuf, was busily hunting for more statues to adorn his villas. An extensive tour of what is now Turkey cemented his passion.

For most scholars, his most important work was probably the seven-volume *Recuiel d'Antiquities,* which appeared at regular intervals from 1752–1767. But Caylus did not spend all of his time cataloguing coins (especially gold coins) and other ancient wonders. He also attended the salons of Paris, still in operation, wrote a number of popular erotic tales, and dabbled in fairy tales and "oriental" tales—that is, tales of magic set in the Middle East, which Caylus, unlike other French writers writing such tales, at least had the benefit of having visited in person.

Caylus wrote decades after Madame d'Aulnoy had pioneered the use of fairy tales as subversive critiques of the court of Louis XIV and after Charles Perrault had used those same fairy tales to uphold the court of Louis XIV—while cautioning children, and in particular girls, of the dangers there. Caylus, familiar with both writers, drove his own path: mocking aspects of the court of Louis XIV, but also adding a touch of misogyny, which both d'Aulnoy and Perrault had largely avoided, and just barely managing to avoid expressing some decidedly negative thoughts about the organization of the French army.

His *Princess Minute and King Floridor,* originally published in 1741, provides an excellent example of this. As the story opens, a large empire has been left to the rule of the tiny, thirteen-year-old Princess Minute, who has a passion for collecting knickknacks, and her fairy protector, Mirdandenne. Shortly after this, Minute dismisses a distinguished general from her court because he wore a hat laced with silver and a coat laced with gold, a negligence that she believes may be a sign of future negligence in battle. These sorts of decisions, Caylus explains, are enough to make anyone—and a kingdom—unstable.

It's not particularly hard to connect all of this to Versailles, with its obsession with manners, fashion, and, well, delicate knickknacks—though it's only fair to note that Caylus himself spent much of his life obsessed with and writing about delicate knickknacks, which may also account for their mention here. But Caylus here is less concerned about expenditures—a decided problem at Versailles, and one that other French salon fairy-tale authors did obliquely or directly address in their tales—than on the absurdity of basing important military matters on trivial things—and also, it seems, on the problem of allowing civilians with no military experience or training to make decisions affecting the military.

Though in this particular case, the princess might have a point: given the court's intense focus on knickknacks and trivia, it would have been prudent for the general to take extra care and—at least for this one appearance—focus on knickknacks and trivia. It sorta reminds me of the time and attention actors take over red-carpet appearances: sure, it's ludicrous, but it's also part of their job. Negligence in one aspect might be linked to negligence elsewhere.

Or, civilian me could be completely wrong, and the former soldier scribing this tale might have been right, and what *really* matters is skill in the battlefield, not what people are wearing on it, or before they reach it.

The story then shifts to the other main character, King Floridor, ruler of a tiny kingdom, whose chief advisor is a charming ant. For those with insect issues who are about to protest that no ant can ever be charming,

I hear you, but this particular ant happens to be a fairy in disguise. When she hears that Minute's kingdom is falling apart thanks to questionable leadership and is about to be invaded by another king interested in marrying Minute, the fairy ant sends Floridor off to rescue Minute—without an army, but with a walnut shell, a little carving knife, and a sparrow.

Minute, meanwhile, is trying to figure out if her troops should wear blue or white cockades. Okay, yes, maybe the earlier criticisms do have a point. She also has failed to build fortifications or stockpile ammunition—something Caylus speaks of with enough exasperation that it seems possible he was thinking of a real-life incident. With no defenses, Floridor believes the only way to save her is to take her back to his own tiny country. Once she's safe, he can return to her country and save it from the invading king.

This part of the tale may have been inspired by any number of historical cases where a queen or an heir fled to another country, leaving others to fight on their behalf. Caylus had met people who had known the exiled Queen Henrietta Maria while she lived in France, for instance, and he may have met Prince Charles Edward Stuart while in Rome. That is, it's realistic—but I also couldn't help remembering other French salon fairy tales where women led armies. Ah well.

Anyway, Minute and Floridor flee, pursued by rebels. Just as the rebel scouts come near them, Floridor accidentally breaks the walnut—revealing a rather convenient army of thirty thousand men. This allows the royal couple to escape—but not for long. They soon find themselves threatened by yet another army. At this point, Minute decides to use the knife for "some trivial purpose." We're never told exactly what that was, leading me to believe that perhaps said purpose was not as trivial as Caylus wants me to believe it was, but when the knife proves to be useless as a regular knife, Minute throws it away—discovering that if it's not particularly good at cutting ordinary things, it *is* good at immediately digging large holes in the ground.

Thanks to this ability to create instant defensive fortifications with the knife, an army that can be carried in a walnut, and a sparrow which turns out to have the ability to lift mountains, Floridor is able to imprison the rebel army inside a mountain and take Minute back to the safety of his own kingdom and the approval of the magic ant. The ant does, however, take the walnut and the knife back—maybe they can only be used a certain number of times?—and sends Floridor back out to war with only a letter from Minute and the sparrow. Fortunately, the sparrow is still up to moving mountains around, which allows Floridor to free the rebel army, gain its support, train its soldiers, and attack the invading king—and win.

It's a fairy-tale ending, of sorts, but not an entirely satisfying one. For one thing, it's rather hard to tell exactly why Floridor is in love with Minute, apart from the fact that they are both in the same story. For another, most of the end of the story is focused on the importance of maintaining order and discipline in military ranks—an important point, and one that clearly nagged at Caylus, but not exactly a traditional part of the fairy-tale ending. Come to think of it, for all that fairy tales often seem obsessed with soldiers and wars, I can't remember another fairy tale quite as determined to stress the importance of military discipline over the particular details of military uniforms.

More importantly, the story ends not with the lovers rejoicing that their troubles are over and ruling their kingdoms happily ever after, but with Minute feeling ashamed that she has done only little things with great help, while her new husband has done great things with little things. This seems more than a bit unfair: a walnut capable of concealing and carrying an *entire army* of thirty thousand men is small only in size but not in consequence, and Minute, not Floridor, was the one to discover how the knife could be used, however accidentally. Of course Floridor accomplished more: he had magical items and a mother who served as his regent until he was old enough to take the throne. Minute ascended her throne at thirteen—an age where a boy might well have been as obsessed with the minutiae of uniforms and gold and silver trim as she was.

And not just unfair, but her sense of shame also seems to be a rather alarming beginning for a marriage. It's hard not to join scholar Jack Zipes in wondering if this tale is not just mocking courtly manners and the frequent shallowness of French courts, but also mocking the very idea of a happy ending—and to a certain degree, even the concept of a fairy tale.

Indeed, for all its criticisms of courtly triviality, its insistence on a professional army, and its various trappings borrowed from earlier tales, *Princess Minute and King Floridor* is less part of the subversive fairy tales of the French salons, and more of a counter-attack on those tales. The aristocratic Caylus does not precisely follow the example of Perrault, whose fairy tales tended to support the court of Versailles, or at least present it as an opportunity for some social climbing. And even in this tale, Caylus offers two examples of women who were able to rule tiny kingdoms, if not large ones It's not entirely as misogynistic as I've made it sound.

But compared to the other French salon fairy tales, it's more than a bit jarring, coming across almost as a statement of "look, I just don't believe you," along with suggesting that really, all a foolish woman needs is a man to organize her life and train and discipline her army. It's notable that the two competent women of the story remain in minor roles and never leave their tiny country, while the two incompetent women play a much larger role in the story, which focuses on their deficiencies. In its attempt to counter the salon fairy-tale stories, it becomes the sort of narrative that reminds us just why many exasperated women turned to writing subversive fairy tales in the first place.

And yet it also serves as an example of the richness of the fairy-tale format: not just in its ability to stretch and accommodate multiple viewpoints, but also in the way it almost demands responses from readers. Caylus had no shortage of material to write about, and no need to earn a living through writing. But he did feel he needed to respond to the fairy-tale writers who preceded him— which says quite a bit about their power.

Unnatural Love and Healing: Charles Perrault's *Donkey-Skin* and Other Fairy Tales

Incestuous and quasi-incestuous relationships were hardly unknown at the court of Louis XIV. The king himself had married his first cousin, Maria-Theresa of Spain, largely for political reasons. His brother Philippe, Duke of Orleans, had married another first cousin, Henrietta of England, before marrying a more distant cousin, Elizabeth Charlotte of the Palatine, whose grandmother was related to the royal French family, and who could trace other connections through both parents. Various aristocrats at the court followed these royal examples for financial or other reasons, and in other countries, the occasional marriage between a niece and uncle, or an aunt and nephew—for political reasons—were not unknown. And those were just the relationships validated by the Church.

That perhaps helps explain why so many of the French salon fairy tales focus on similar relationships between cousins or even closer relations and why Charles Perrault decided to take up the theme in what is often regarded as the least pleasant of his fairy tales, *Donkey-Skin,* classified by folklorists as Aarne-Thompson type 510B, unnatural love.

Perrault may have borrowed portions of his tale from Apuleius's second-century tale of *Cupid and Psyche*, also a source for *Beauty and the Beast* and *East o' the Sun, West o' the Moon* and "The Singing, Springing Lark." But as with his *Sleeping Beauty in the Wood*, a more direct source was Giambattista Basile, and his tale "The She-Bear" collected in his 1634 *The Pentamerone, or The Story of Stories*.

As in pretty much *any* story by Basile, this one can be basically summed up with "horrific," "cruel," and "over the top," though it's fair to say that it's not anywhere close to the most horrific story in the collection. It is also the *only* version of the story where arguably the incest is not the most alarming or problematic part of the tale. It starts with a beautiful, dying queen, who tells her husband that he must not marry unless he can find a bride as beautiful as she, and continues with a scene of every woman in the kingdom and several women beyond the kingdom lining up for the king's inspection, not at all incidentally giving Basile the opportunity to say a number of excessively mean-spirited things about the looks of all women so unfortunate as to be born outside Italy, and more specifically, Naples. Not that Basile exactly had an overly high opinion of Italy, and more specifically, Naples; he just had an even worse opinion of everything outside Italy, and more specifically, Naples.

Oh, sure, the woman from Naples *also* gets turned down—but only because she's wearing high-heeled shoes. The women not from Naples all have various physical defects.

Anyway, insult time over, the king eventually decides that the only woman who can meet the qualification is his daughter. Fortunately, an old woman just happens to have a little piece of wood that can turn the daughter into a bear. (I must note that none of the old women I meet ever have things like this. It seems very unfair.) The daughter—Prezioza—escapes into the woods. Where, of course, she meets a prince.

While she is still a bear.

I feel that once again I should let Bazile tell the story from here:

> "Mother, my lady, if I don't give this bear a kiss, my last breath will leave me!"
>
> The queen, who saw that he was about to faint, said, "Kiss him, kiss him, my lovely animal, don't let me see this poor son of mine perish!"
>
> The bear went over to him, and the prince grabbed her cheeks and couldn't get enough of kissing her.

MOVING ON. The bear, I should note, turns out to be one awesome servant—adding a nice touch of sexual harassment and a bit of a power imbalance to the bestiality, like, as said, the incest? Arguably NOT THE WORST PART HERE—largely because the bear remembers to strew flowers everywhere, which is a surprisingly nice touch given the rest of the invective here.

It all ends with literal fireworks.

Perrault prudently decided to leave out any speculation about human/bear relationships, instead choosing to start his story with, well a donkey. A rather magical donkey, who has earned the highest of donkey accolades: a splendid stall. Indeed, the most splendid stall in what appears to be the virtual definition of "luxury stable."

Perrault soon reveals the reason for this: every night, bushels of gold coins spill from its ears in the sanitized English translation of the tale, or from a less comfortable location in the digestive system in the original French version.

Once again I have questions. Like, yes, I realize this is the 17th century, not exactly renowned for quality veterinary services, but has *anyone* checked to see what physical condition might be causing this? Or worried that this sort of thing—whether going through the ears or through the digestive system—might be causing the donkey some pain? I mean, speaking just in general, and in as ungross a way as possible, traditionally, ears and colons have not been used to store gold for rather good reasons. Is this all a way for the donkey to convert straw to gold, like Rumpelstiltskin, and if so, did anyone consider handing the donkey a spinning wheel to see if a less painful method might work? And if you're about to tell me, *Yes, but donkeys can't spin*, true, but usually, donkeys? Not capable of this sort of digestive activity.

And on a practical level, is keeping this donkey in a beautiful, plush stall without any particular explanation *really* the best way of keeping the donkey's abilities secret from the general public? I mean, yes, I understand wanting to keep the donkey as happy as possible to ensure that he doesn't run away, but the story is pretty clear on this: visitors to the stables are definitely asking questions. This is not a very secure donkey, is what I'm saying.

In any case, the king soon has much bigger problems: his beloved wife is dying, and worse, she's putting conditions on what happens after her death. The king must marry again—a sensible command, not just because they apparently don't have a son, but because, as we're about to see, he's not exactly the most mentally stable monarch making it a *very* good idea to have a potential regent/co-ruler hanging around—but he can only marry a woman more beautiful than she.

A quick glance at the portraits of many 17th-century princesses might suggest that this would not be not all *that* difficult of a task—the king just needs to marry someone who isn't, well, a princess. This is, however, a fairy tale, which likes to pretend that 17th-century French queens and princesses *were* beautiful and not just beautifully dressed, whatever their portraits might suggest, leaving the king kinda stuck.

But he does have a daughter. An adopted daughter, in the sanitized English translation later published by Andrew Lang in *The Grey Fairy Book* (1900).

His actual daughter, in the original French (1695).

More beautiful than any of the portraits sent his way.

To be fair, see what I said above about many 17th-century princesses.

To be less fair, the king decides that the only way he can fulfill his late wife's command is by marrying his own daughter.

The girl, not surprisingly, is horrified. Like many other French salon fairy-tale princesses, she turns immediately to her fairy godmother for aid. This one, rather than offering a magical item, or removing her to safety, or doing anything remotely *useful*, instead suggests that the princess ask her father for a dress that matches the sky, assuring the girl that the king can't possibly do this. Again, I have questions, in this case mostly about the fairy godmother, and specifically: has she *seen* the French court? Or any paintings of the French court? Louis XIV was very very into clothes, is what I'm saying, and if he demanded a dress that matched the sky, he could easily get a dress that matched the sky. This might have been less possible in another court, but in that time and in a fairy tale—well.

The king finds the dress. The girl returns to her fairy godmother. Still stuck on fashion, the godmother suggests that the girl ask for a dress of moonbeams and then for a dress of sunshine. None of this stops the king. Finally, the godmother suggests that the girl ask for the skin of that magical donkey, assuming that the king will never want to give up the source of his wealth.

Once again, the godmother is wrong.

The girl, defeated, slinks out of the palace, hidden in the donkey skin.

You will perhaps not be surprised at this point to find out that the fairy godmother has kinda forgotten to provide her with any *money*, forcing the girl to hunt for work, which is a problem, not so much because of her lack of work experience (though that couldn't have been helpful) but because, well, she's wearing a donkey skin, which even in the 17th-century was not considered appropriate attire for a job interview. Especially a donkey skin which hasn't been cleaned yet or at all and apparently still has some blood and other stains, like, yuck, and girl, I know you're fleeing from an understandably *very* unwanted marriage, but, really. Soap can be your friend. Eventually, however, she is able to find a job at a farm where they are willing to let her take care of the pigs and turkeys. It all works out.

Perrault, remember, worked his way up the social ladder, leaving him with the firm belief that, yes, hard work could and would lead to social advancement—a message he generally delivered through the figures of fantastically beautiful heroines, but I anticipate.

Anyway, all goes well, until, that is, the girl sees her reflection, and realizes just how terrible the donkey skin looks. WELL MAYBE IF YOU HAD TAKEN THE TIME TO CLEAN IT IN THE FIRST PLACE YOU WOULDN'T BE IN THIS SITUATION, but rather than thinking about this, she instead decides it's about time to take a bath, which WELL YES, and the experience makes her decide that she needs to be a princess whenever she can, even if this is only in her room.

(Disney! In general, not your sort of tale, but I do sense a potential ad campaign idea for Disney Princesses here!)

Which is what she's doing when a prince just happens to peek through the keyhole of her room, seeing her in her sunshine dress.

It drives him into a high fever, which, he announces, can only be cured by eating a cake made by Donkey-Skin. Look, 17th-century medicine had its limitations. The girl drops her ring into the cake—Perrault carefully adds that this might or might not be an accidental sort of drop—nearly choking the prince.

And every girl in the kingdom is summoned to try on the ring—which fits only the girl.

Their wedding, incidentally, is attended by people who arrive riding tigers and eagles, which is kinda *awesome* and also probably a nice nod to the various exotic animals sent as gifts to Louis XIV.

Perrault originally published the story in verse form in 1695, and then included it two years later in his *Histories ou contes du temps passé,* a collection that also included his more famous stories of *Cinderella, Sleeping Beauty, Puss in Boots, Little Red Riding Hood*, and *Bluebeard.* A few of these stories later found themselves inserted into the Grimm collection, in slightly altered form. The same may have happened in this case, with *Allerleirauh*, better known in English as *All Kinds of Fur*, collected by the Grimms from Dorchen Wild, who later married Wilhelm Grimm.

As with *Donkey-Skin, Allerleirauh/All Kinds of Fur* tells the tale of a dying queen who demands that the king remarry a woman more beautiful than she. As with *Donkey-Skin, Allerleirauh/All Kinds of Fur*, the king finds that the only woman who matches this description is his own daughter. And once again, the daughter demands three dresses—like the sun, the moon, and the stars—and a coat of fur before she will marry him. As with her predecessor, once she receives these items, she flees, cloaks herself in the fur, and finds refuge working as a low-end servant in a castle kitchen. And, as with *Donkey-Skin*, the heroine "accidentally" drops golden objects into the king's food, allowing the king to find her.

But the stories have some significant differences as well. In *Allerleirauh/All Kinds of Fur*, the courtiers are *horrified* by the king's plan. In *Donkey-Skin*, they are silent. We do hear from the terrified dressmakers, but never from the courtiers. In *Donkey-Skin*, the girl turns to a fairy godmother for aid. In *Allerleirauh/All Kinds of Fur*, perhaps aware that that an earlier fairy godmother was completely useless, the girl conceives of her demands herself. And she doesn't simply hide in her room, wearing her glorious dresses; she flings off her cloak formed of a thousand furs and proudly attends the ball. Not for long, but she does attend. She deliberately drops golden objects into the king's food to gain his attention. And the king does not need to force all of the maidens of the kingdom to try on a ring. All he needs to do is seize her hand, forcing her cloak to shift just enough to show off her dress—revealing who she really is. All in all, with one minor exception, this later protagonist holds far more power—not surprising, perhaps, given that her tale was told by a woman, and *Donkey-Skin* by a man.

That one exception? Allerleirauh is taken to the king's palace to work in the kitchen after hiding in a tree; Donkey-Skin makes her way to the king's farm on her own two feet. But Allerleirauh was doing quite well for herself before this, without the help of any fairy godmothers, managing not to starve. And in *Allerleirauh/All Kinds of Fur*, the girl's father vanishes after she leaves the palace. At the end of *Donkey-Skin,* the girl's father attends her wedding. Oh, he's been married since—but she is unable to escape him entirely.

And the second tale, of course, has no donkeys, magical or otherwise.

It's possible that Wild had read or heard some version of *Donkey-Skin* before she told her version to the Grimms. But it's equally possible that Dorchen Wild derived her story from other older stories—including "The She-Bear."

It's not at all surprising that Wild, the Grimms, and Perrault decided to leave the bestiality element out of their retellings, emphasizing that their princes and kings fell in love with the *girl*, not her beastly skin. Or that Andrew Lang, while deciding to collect both tales, would choose a softened version of *Donkey-Skin* in *The Grey Fairy Book*. (Apparently, the comparative independence and power of the heroine of *Allerleirauh/All Kinds of Fur*, as well as the horror shown by other characters to the incest of the tale, was enough to save that version from severe editing.) Or that the basics of the story appear in many other folklore traditions and fairy tales, less known, but still poignant.

But it is, perhaps, somewhat surprising that this story, in nearly all of its versions, so often gets classified as a Cinderella story. Oh, both tales often have similar elements: unpleasant housework, a girl whose beauty is hidden beneath a disguise of dirt and fur (or, in the case of "The She-Bear," an actual bear transformation), a need to escape a home, a ball, and an item of clothing that only fits the girl, though notably not all of these elements are present in all versions.

But I think the differences are even more significant. For one thing, in *Donkey-Skin* and its variants, housework is generally a *salvation*, not a punishment, directly leading heroines not just to princes and kings and princes with really strong feelings about bears, but also to food and shelter and above all, *safety* from their fathers. For another thing, in most variants, Cinderella does not choose her rags and dirt: they are imposed on her by her stepmother. Donkey-Skin and her sisters choose their rags, dirt, and animal skins as disguises—sometimes hated disguises, but disguises. In Cinderella and its variants, the danger usually comes from other women, and the heroine is helped by magic (her own, or that granted by a fairy godmother) and a prince. Donkey-Skin and her sisters are usually threatened by men and helped and protected by women; the magic of their tales is generally not all that helpful until the girls escape.

I do not think it a coincidence that a woman gets Donkey-Skin the job at a royal farm, or that the queen is the one able to bring the bear into the palace and convince the bear to kiss the prince. *Cinderella* is a story of power, of social-climbing, of escaping poverty into wealth. *Donkey-Skin* is a story of how wealth may not always protect you from powerful men, of escaping that wealth to hide in poverty before achieving it again.

And it is also a tale of how some women respond to abuse: through transformation, flight, and hard work.

For all of its happy endings, it is not an easy tale, or a tale with easy answers. Nor does it offer a hope of fairy godmothers and magical rescues—even the transformed bear has to fight her way out of her home. But for all of its trauma, and uneasy subject matter, to put it mildly, it does offer hope that abuse and evil can be escaped and overcome, and even lead to triumph.

MARIE CATHERINE LE JUMEL
DE BERNEVILLE.
Comtesse d'Aulnoi.
Morte au Mois de Janvier 1705.

Elizabeth Cheron Pinx   *Bassan Sculp*

Marie-Catherine Le Jumel de Barneville,
Comtesse d'Aulnoy

A Transformed Woman:
Madame d'Aulnoy's *The White Cat*

"Either become a woman, or make me a cat."

The image of a beast hiding deep within an enchanted forest in an enchanted castle, waiting to be transformed through love, is generally associated with, well, *male* beasts. The beasts also typically have a frightening appearance: they are often bears, or lions, or something too terrifying to describe.

But sometimes, that enchanted beast is a girl. As in Madame d'Aulnoy's novelette, *The White Cat*.

Marie-Catherine Le Jumel de Barneville, Comtesse d'Aulnoy, (1650–1705) lived a life that was either mostly fabulous or mostly fabricated, depending on precisely whom you spoke to. One of those fabulous fabrications: accusing her husband of committing high treason, an allegation that eventually forced her to flee France for a time. Despite her exile, she later purchased a house in Paris in the late 1680s, without her estranged husband's assistance but with his at least tacit permission, and established a literary salon that in turn helped establish the passion for the elaborate French salon fairy tales.

D'Aulnoy's tales, designed to entertain an audience for at least a couple of hours, tended to be long, intricate, and highly political, typically specifically focusing on the way aristocratic regimes—not to mention Louis XIV *specifically*—frequently entrapped aristocratic women, leaving them unable to choose their own fortunes and careers. This was equally true for less aristocratic women, but D'Aulnoy's tales show little if any interest in the problems of the lower classes. Or men. She was fixated on aristocratic women, as *The White Cat* shows.

The White Cat opens with an aging king terrified that his three brave and handsome sons are about to overthrow him and take over his kingdom, not an entirely unknown or unrealistic threat during d'Aulnoy's life. The king decides that his best bet is to make use of something straight out of fairy tales—send all three sons on long, largely frivolous quests to ensure that they are too distracted to plot revolution. His first request: find a cute dog, promising that whichever son finds the cutest dog will get the kingdom.

All three of them set out to look for cute dogs. I would not have thought that finding a cute dog would be all that difficult, but then again, I like dogs, and as this story is about to demonstrate, most of the characters in this tale are really more cat people. D'Aulnoy assures us that the oldest two sons had various dog-hunting adventures, but in pure fairy-tale fashion, she chooses to ignore the oldest two and instead focus on the youngest.

Also in pure fairy-tale fashion, this youngest prince is of course ideal: handsome, well mannered, cheerful, and brave. He even has—this is spelled out in the tale—excellent teeth, ensuring that the rest of the story will be free from dental issues. That said, I must say that, for all of d'Aulnoy's efforts to get me on the side of this prince, and to get me to recognize this prince as the most accomplished, most charming, and most astonishing prince ever, it does not exactly take much for her to turn me completely against this prince; as part of this Quest for the Perfect Dog, the prince keeps buying new dogs, then *letting the old dogs go* every time he finds a new, apparently better/more charming dog. Which is, again according to the text, about 30,000 adorable dogs thinking that they finally had a human at last, only to be abandoned a few days later, which seems horrifically harsh on the dogs. So, I'm against this prince from the start.

Anyway. While dog-hunting, the prince happens upon an exquisitely beautiful palace in the forest, as fairy-tale characters do, leaving the rest of us gloomily looking at our GPS devices and wishing we'd brought along more chocolate for this forest expedition. Moving on. Naturally, he enters the castle, which equally naturally is staffed by invisible singing servants—that is, invisible right up to the moment where disembodied hands start to undress and then dress him. Ugh. After this the hands escort him to dinner—a dinner where the music is composed of cat meows (considerably less tuneful than the later songs in Disney's *Aristocats*) and where his companion is a beautiful little white talking cat.

SPOILER ALERT this is an enchanted castle.

The delighted prince spends a year there, forgetting everything else, and, perhaps most importantly from my point of view, *stops looking for dogs* and thus ending their torture, which, come to think of it, may have been the plan of the cats all along. I mean, sure, cats aren't always known for their goodwill toward dogs, but some cats and some dogs have become friends, and I have to assume that even the most hard-hearted cat would have felt terrible about the dog issue. Moving on. At the end of the year, the white cat sends him back home, with a tiny dog concealed in an acorn.

The other two princes have also found dogs (it's not clear if they, too, abandoned several other dogs along the way), but their admittedly adorable and beautiful dogs can't exactly compete with a tiny dog capable of doing a Spanish dance. The king, meanwhile, decides to send the princes out yet again—this time on a hunt for fine cloth. The prince returns to the white cat and spends another enchanted year with her, departing with the cloth hidden in yet another nut. The king ups the requirements a third time: forget cute dogs or fine cloth, they need to bring back a beautiful maiden. The prince, not surprisingly, decides to spend another year with his cat.

At the end of that year, the cat asks him to cut off her head.

This, as it turns out, is the start of a second tale—a story of a princess trapped in a tower thanks to the foolish whims and demands of her mother, a princess who defiantly marries a king without permission from her guardians and finds herself and the aristocrats in her palace transformed into cats until she finds a man who looks exactly like that king.

The White Cat is not exactly original. Its themes, motifs, and basic plots, both of the "enchanted cat" and the "princess in a tower," can be found in numerous other stories, many—perhaps most—better written. The introduction of a story within a story in the second half feels more than a bit unwieldy—to the point where several English translations have left it out entirely, just skipping from the cat beheading to the last few paragraphs.

Plot holes are abundant, and certain details remain inexplicable—not least, the questions of just why getting transformed into a *beautiful* cat capable of granting virtually every request on earth is such a terrible fate, and also, what happened to the tiny dog in the acorn, and also, just how does this prince resemble the king so exactly? Were they somehow related? Or did some kind—or practical—fairy realize that the cat had been punished enough already, or was presenting far too much of a drain on the fairy resources, what with all of the magical weaving and the summoning of jewels and the creation of cat orchestras, and really, it was best for everyone to make a prince look like the former king.

Not to mention that the original problem presented by the story—who, exactly, is going to take control of the kingdom—never really does get solved.

I suspect, too, that for many people, the "Oh, you got transformed into a cat and now have to live a life of endless enchanted luxury waited on by mostly invisible servants, with no need to work, ever, and with your only companions other cats capable of writing poetry and novels" is not *exactly* the worst sort of punishment they can envision. I'll be honest. It sounds like precisely my ideal life, and I was not exactly surprised—nor baffled—to see the prince begging to be transformed into a cat. Which is to say, I'm having a hard time with the "SAVE ME, PRINCE, BY CUTTING OFF MY HEAD" deal here. No, Princess. Remain a cat. Take a lot of naps in between snacking on things. Life could be much worse.

Also, this prince? Does less than anyone else in any fairy tale, ever, to earn his happy ending. I mean, he abandons a lot of adorable dogs, rides a horse, uses other people's labor to argue that he should win his brother's throne, spends three years delighting in life at an enchanted castle, and cuts off the head of a cat. That's—yeah, that's it.

And it's more than a touch disturbing to realize that the men trapped as beasts can be saved through marriage, extensive traveling, and massive sacrifice on the part of the women, and a kiss, while the girl trapped as a cat can only be rescued through sudden violence.

It is a not particularly subtle comment on the issues faced by aristocratic women in d'Aulnoy's day. D'Aulnoy had no way of ridding herself of a deeply unwanted husband: she had to wait for death to remove that obstacle. But she also saw men rescue themselves through using the financial resources of wealthy women, usually through marriage—as the prince does in this story, and watched men imprison their wives for small offenses—as a side character does in this story. The women in this story find themselves trapped in towers and enchanted palaces unable to rescue people about to be sacrificed to dragons. The men travel around freely, occasionally eaten by dragons (okay, *once*), but for the most part able to make their own choices—and more than once, make the choices that affect the women.

But for me, at least, the power of the story stems less from its critiques of aristocratic French society (not exactly the most sympathetic group in history), but from the little details. Like the throwaway line that royal princes were expected to be able to perform music *and* paint. (This may well have been intended as a nasty crack at the ruling Bourbon family, whose members were better known for patronizing art than for creating it.) Or the other throwaway line suggesting that magical castles are decorated with images inspired by other fairy tales, which, let's just say it, is *marvelous.* Especially since many of the fairy tales mentioned were d'Aulnoy's kind nods to other authors. Or the little side scene of the prince managing to earn a pardon for four cats who conspired with—I hope you're prepared for the horror—*two rats,* to eat food meant for the dinner of the white cat (If you weren't prepared for that horror, I'm sorry), a side scene that allowed d'Aulnoy to make another graceful nod to fellow author and poet Jean de la Fontaine. The way the fairies ensure that this princess in a tower gets to have a parrot and a dog to make sure she's not all that lonely.

The length and structure of *The White Cat* presumably explains why it never really achieved the popularity of other French salon fairy tales, although Andrew Lang collected a translation for his *The Blue Fairy Book* (1889) and multiple translations are widely available online. But if it never achieved the popularity of *Cinderella*, it did make its own, forthright statements about women—and helped establish the genre of the French salon fairy tales. An impressive achievement for a woman able to see the restrictions and traps created by her society.

About the Author

Born in Massachusetts, Mari Ness spent much of her life wandering the world and reading, which trained her to do one thing in life: write. Her interest in fairy tales was first sparked by a gloriously illustrated book given to her as a birthday present when she was four, and solidified by a later book of Italian fairy tales which were even better, because they included a funny talking parrot. She continued to hunt down as many tales as she could. She holds a degree in English and medieval studies from the University at Binghamton, and has done additional graduate work in history and marine biology. More than one hundred of her short stories have appeared in multiple publications including *Clarkesworld*, *Tor.com*, *Lightspeed*, *Uncanny*, *Fireside*, *Nightmare*, *Diabolical Plots*, *Daily Science Fiction*, *Capricious SF*, and *Kaleidotrope*. Her poetry has appeared in *Strange Horizons*, *The Mithila Review*, *Twisted Moon*, *Polu Texni*, and *Goblin Fruit* and has been nominated for the Rhysling, Dwarf Stars, and Elgin Awards. She is also the author of *Through Immortal Shadows Singing*, a novella in poetry. She currently lives in central Florida, where she watches terrible TV, reads considerably less terrible books, and dreams of one day making the yard worthy of a fairy tale.